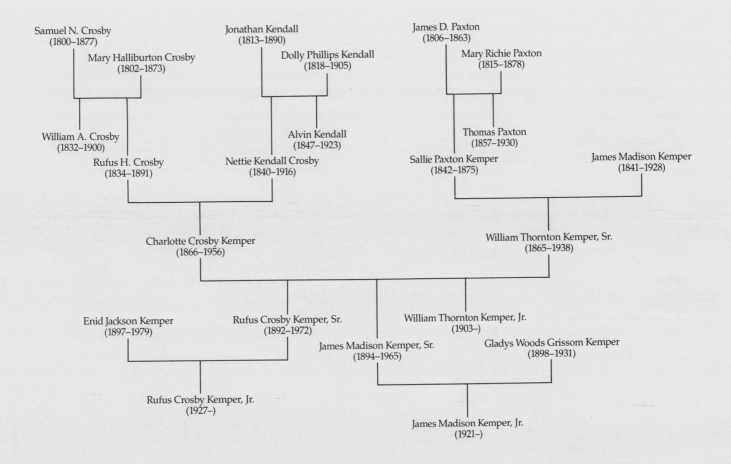

Samuel N. Crosby
(1800–1877)

Mary Halliburton Crosby
(1802–1873)

Jonathan Kendall
(1813–1890)

Dolly Phillips Kendall
(1818–1905)

James D. Paxton
(1806–1863)

Mary Richie Paxton
(1815–1878)

William A. Crosby
(1832–1900)

Alvin Kendall
(1847–1923)

Thomas Paxton
(1857–1930)

Rufus H. Crosby
(1834–1891)

Nettie Kendall Crosby
(1840–1916)

Sallie Paxton Kemper
(1842–1875)

James Madison Kemper
(1841–1928)

Charlotte Crosby Kemper
(1866–1956)

William Thornton Kemper, Sr.
(1865–1938)

Enid Jackson Kemper
(1897–1979)

Rufus Crosby Kemper, Sr.
(1892–1972)

William Thornton Kemper, Jr.
(1903–)

James Madison Kemper, Sr.
(1894–1965)

Gladys Woods Grissom Kemper
(1898–1931)

Rufus Crosby Kemper, Jr.
(1927–)

James Madison Kemper, Jr.
(1921–)

Building a
First Class Bank

Courtyard in the new Kansas City headquarters of United Missouri Bancshares

THE STORY OF UNITED MISSOURI BANK

By
BRENT SCHONDELMEYER

PUBLISHED BY UNITED MISSOURI BANCSHARES, INC.
KANSAS CITY, MISSOURI

*This book is dedicated to an ideal—that of being a first-class bank—
and to all the customers, shareholders, directors, officers, and associates
whose dreams, ambitions, and hard work have made it possible. It is their
collective story; it has been our singular success.*

Contents

Joseph Bogart,
oil, 36x28 in.,
Rembrandt Peale

vii

From the Collection of
UNITED MISSOURI BANCSHARES

**George Washington Leaving for Mount Vernon
After His Resignation from U.S. Military,**
oil, 30x40 in.,
E. Percy Moran

Foreword

My memory of the United Missouri Bank goes back to two other names: the City National Bank and, even before that, to a predecessor called the City Center Bank, located on the west side of Grand Avenue across from the Kansas City Star Building in World War I days.

These enterprises have thrived beyond imagination because of excellent management through the generations. Both Kempers—Crosby, Sr. and Crosby, Jr.—have had two characteristics in common: a rare understanding of credit and a zeal for hard work.

But, perhaps, my extreme fondness for both men stems from their deep understanding of human nature and their irrepressible sense of humor. In my memory, they stand out as engaging companions and consummate storytellers, always delightful to be with.

It has been a privilege to be a part of the wonderful institution they have created. My life and the lives of all Kansas Citians have been immeasurably enriched by these two outstanding human beings.

HERMAN R. SUTHERLAND
Managing Partner
Sutherland Lumber Company

Mrs. Joseph Kinney,
(1874) oil, 25x20 in.,
George Caleb Bingham

One of the great observers of the American scene during this century was Pulitzer-prize-winning journalist William Allen White. The Emporia, Kansas, journalist had gained widespread acclaim for telling the nation "What's the Matter with Kansas?" but he also had strong ideas about what was right with his nation, particularly that great section known as the Midwest. In White's opinion, the United States was a great nation because of men like William Kemper, whose creation of a banking empire made his boyhood ambition to become a shoe salesman seem pitifully insignificant. When the Kansas City banker died in 1938, White wrote of his friend: "In the last 300 years in this country there have been 10,000 Kempers, all built on the same pattern — great diligence, indomitable purpose, broad imagination which is called vision when it is directed by wisdom, and upon an essential American kind of heart. Upon men of this kind America has depended for her progress. They have been the bone and sinew of this land."

Ostensibly, this book tells of the growth of a Kansas City bank from a one-room storefront bank, founded in 1913, into one of the Midwest's most successful and profitable banking concerns — United Missouri Bancshares, Inc. However, the chronicle is incomplete without telling the more personal story of three generations of Kansas City bankers for whom William Kemper served as the family patriarch to be emulated by his sons and grandsons. Though he had not graduated from high school, Kemper taught the boys lessons from the school of hard knocks that were well remembered, such as "Find out what a man's made of. A person's character means more than his financial statement." Kemper believed that the character of a family member was no less important than that of a bank customer; and he worked hard to instill strong character in his sons by consistently conveying to them through word and action the value of hard work, community involvement, and a commitment to excellence.

This is the story of one family's influence in shaping the growth and development of an important banking institution and its home community, Kansas City. The narrative begins prior to the Civil War when two brothers from Maine, Rufus and William Crosby, moved to eastern Kansas where they started a dry-goods business and willingly accepted "coon skins, but-

Captain Joseph Kinney,
(1874) oil, 30x25 in.,
George Caleb Bingham

Lady with the Mulberries,
oil, 41x37 in.,
Henry Benbridge

ter, beef hides, cheese, potatoes" as payment. Eventually, Rufus left the dry-goods business to go into banking. United Missouri traces its history back to his private bank in Valley Falls, Kansas, where William Kemper learned the basic tenets of banking while working for his father-in-law Rufus Crosby.

These two banks are worlds apart, separated by a century and a major revolution within the banking industry involving credit cards, electronic fund transfers, computers, central banking, and government regulation. The tie that binds the two banks, over and above family ties, is a philosophy expressed in the public commitment Rufus Crosby made when he opened his bank in 1879: "Our steady purpose shall be to do all the various and legitimate kinds of business of a **First Class Bank,** on strict and true banking rules and regulations." Over the years, that concept has been conveyed to thousands of men and women who have worked for United Missouri Bancshares and have contributed to building it into one of the finest banking organizations in the nation.

United Missouri Bancshares is a successful banking company, and each year its annual report yields the largely impersonal statistics — earnings, return on assets, equity and liquidity ratios — that bring a glimmer to a financial analyst's eye and nodding approval. The impressive numbers tend to gloss over the fundamental proposition that, above all else, banking is a personal business; and that facet of the bank's success, most assuredly, is attributable to the strong personality of William Kemper, who knew the value and enjoyed the rewards of being able to "teach his children well."

The lessons he taught were not merely about banking, but about the importance of believing in one's self, motivating others to do their best, and working hard for the betterment of the community. They remain instructive lessons for us all.

~/~

Rufus Crosby

BANKING ON THE PRAIRIE

One of the remaining relics of the Valley Falls Bank of Deposit is an old square-screw-door money safe still in use in the successor bank. The 2,000-pound safe, built by the well-known Mosler Safe Company, can be opened only by using a combination and then rotating a big crank a turn and a half. The design was intended to thwart bank robbers in the late 1800s who were using nitro-glycerin to blow off safe doors. The laminated plate-steel safe dating from the 1880s cost approximately $100.

"Our banking institutions are a source of accommodation that our people cannot do without. We are not of those who look upon banks as only sources of evil . . . but believe them to be just as necessary and just as great a source of accommodation as a store for the sale of any other commodity."

Kansas New Era, *April 1876*
Valley Falls, Kansas

The word up and down main street in January of 1878 was that the private bank of Mark P. Hillyer was in serious trouble. Word did not have far to travel. By the time the dry-goods merchant told the farmer, who informed his wife, who told the other women at church, nearly everyone on the Kansas plains around the small farming town of Valley Falls knew that its leading bank at the corner of Broadway and Sycamore had problems.

Founded in 1871, Valley Bank and Savings Institution had weathered the national financial crash of 1873 and the local agricultural disaster the following year when drought and grasshoppers took their toll. However, by January 1878, confidence in the bank was shaky partly because of the lack of trust placed in Hillyer, an Ohio-born farmer. Mounting rumors of a run on the bank were causing the directors to fear that the bank's reserves might be depleted.

Up the street from the bank, dry-goods merchants Rufus Crosby and Alvin Kendall were quite conversant with the bank's affairs. Rufus's brother William was a bank stockholder and one-time bank vice-president. Moreover, the two merchants—who were brothers-in-law—knew for themselves that hard times and liberal lending had contributed to the bank's problems. Working from behind the counter of their store, the two transplanted New Englanders also had their customers as a crude gauge of the local economy. How many customers paid cash? How many needed credit? Could their customers afford notions purchased from New York or did their shopping lists contain only the bare essentials?

In August of 1878, the Valley Falls newspaper reported: "The Topeka National Bank closed its doors Monday morning. The lightning struck this time within twenty-five miles of Valley Falls." Lightning striking so close to Valley Falls intensified rumors about Valley Bank and Savings Institution, which caused Rufus Crosby to ruminate about the prospects of becoming a banker. Then on January 27, 1879, Valley Bank and Savings Institution closed its doors; and Rufus quickly formulated plans to establish a new bank. The February 1, 1879, issue of the *Valley Falls New Era* carried a long formal announcement by the two dry-goods merchants that informed the public of the name, the owners, the philosophy, and the policies of a new bank, which

they intended to call Crosby and Kendall's Valley Falls Bank of Deposit:

Rufus Crosby, Valley Falls, Kansas, about 1880

"We propose to start a new Bank with the above name, in this city. In these days of misplaced confidence in bank accounts, when even honest purposes frequently fail of being crystallized into *bona fide* performance, the first question as our new project strikes the public ear, will be, is it **Solid**?

"In answer, we will give a truthful, though unsworn statement. The head of our banking concern (junior of Crosby Bros. in '56) will personally and specially attend to the management of this bank. To the success of this enterprise he pledges, without reserve, all his property, every dollar of which is in his own name and unencumbered.

"Here is a bank where depositors may place their funds with a sense of relief and repose, in safe custody, and at a moderate rate of interest. It is, in our opinion, *prima facie* evidence of unsoundness and distress for a bank to pay a high rate of interest on deposits. We would prefer to put surplus funds of this Bank in government 4 percent bonds (where they could be speedily made available in case of emergency), than to invest them at a high and flattering rate in speculative and uncertain securities.

"We respectfully solicit your patronage but will frankly tell you at the outset, that, should you offer for discount any paper that we consider shaky, we shall not hesitate to say No, gracefully as the circumstances will allow, but with all the stubbornness of fate itself.

"Our views on the proper theory of banking, can be briefly stated thus: As much individual responsibility, at least, should be required to start a bank, as to open a store, or run a grist-mill.

"The fault, not to say fraud, on the 'joint Stock Banking System,' that has proven so disastrous during the last decade, is that it permits an incorporated company—clothed with all the respectability of State Law—to proclaim a Capital of $100,000 or more, when the actual cash basis may not be over $10,000, or even less.

"In closing, we will add that we are heartily in accord with the 'Resumption Policy' and thoroughly believe that no individual as well as government, has any moral or financial right to attempt to float more paper than can be kept at par with gold.

"Our steady purpose shall be to do all the various and legitimate kinds of business of a **First Class Bank**, on strict and true banking rules and regulations."

Offices of the newly opened bank were in the counting room of the dry-goods store for a week until Rufus Crosby bought the "building, fixtures and goodwill" of Valley Bank and Savings Institution and moved his bank to the two-story corner brick building one block east of the store. Rufus publicly announced that his Valley Falls Bank of Deposit had $50,000 in capital, adding "Your accounts solicited without fear or favor." Wanting to devote full time to banking, the forty-four-year-old Rufus sold his interest in the dry-goods store to his brother-in-law Alvin Kendall, who had decided not to go into the banking business.

In 1879, Valley Falls was an established community approaching twenty-five years old. Rufus H. Crosby, who had been a teacher, frontier newspaper editor, politician, and retail merchant, had become the town's newest banker. He had already witnessed much during his quarter century on the plains: the border war between proslavery advocates and abolitionists in Kansas; the admission of the territory into the Union during the ensuing Civil War; the coming of rail lines through the town; the introduction of

winter wheat into the state by German-Russian immigrants; and the growth of his adopted state.

William and Rufus Crosby were the second and third children born to the marriage of Samuel Crosby and Mary Halliburton on their small family farm in Hampden, Maine. Rufus was born on October 5, 1834. The following week the family celebrated William's second birthday. By the time this fourth generation of Hampden, Maine, Crosbys was born, the Scottish-English clan was quite prominent in the community. Simon Crosby—great-grandfather of William and Rufus—had first moved his family to Hampden in 1773 from Woolwich, Maine. He had brought with him his wife Sarah and ten children. An eleventh child had been born the next year.

Life in Hampden revolved around lumbering and shipbuilding, as the hamlet was at the head of the navigable reaches of the Penobscot River. The town grew steadily with the Crosbys deeply involved in its progress. The children from the large clan of Crosbys became the town's lumbermen, farmers, shipbuilders, soldiers, and merchants. The family of Rufus and William Crosby turned to the land, not the sea, for their livelihood. Their grandfather Ebenezer taught the boys' father Samuel to till the land on a 100-acre lot that he owned on North Main Street, less than a mile from the river. Samuel Crosby, in turn, was aided by his two older sons William and Rufus

Young Lady of the Motte Family, *oil, 35½x27½ in., Jeremiah Theus*

in running their East Hampden farm. Working on the farm held little promise for the two Crosby brothers. Young men of ambition increasingly looked westward, drawn by the 1848 discovery of gold in California.

Rufus was too young to look for gold. Instead he searched the pages of his textbooks for knowledge at the Hampden Academy. A good student, Rufus himself became a teacher and worked two terms at common schools in the area, while most of his friends returned to work on family farms. William was the first to leave the family farm around 1851, when he traveled to southern Illinois and got a job working as a topographer for an engineer in charge of building the Illinois Central Railway. In 1854, Rufus left Maine and moved to Minneapolis, Minnesota, where William joined him. The brothers left for the Kansas territory in 1855, citing the cold Minnesota winters as the reason for moving south. The Crosby brothers, like other New Englanders who had migrated to the territory to oppose slavery, quickly embraced the passions and fervor of Kansas politics.

William and Rufus moved to Atchison County and helped to settle a new town on Stranger Creek named Oceana, an unlikely name for a town a thousand miles inland from the Atlantic. Oceana, sometimes spelled Ocena, was located at the intersection of the Saint Joseph-Topeka stage line, ten miles west of Atchison, a major Missouri River town. The Crosby brothers ran a small store, and William was the postmaster.

When elections were held for a territorial legislature in March of 1855, bands of armed Missourians crossed the border into the Kansas territory to vote in the election and to deny free-state settlers living in Kansas the opportunity to vote. The free-state forces dubbed the newly elected body the "Bogus Legislature" and decided to hold separate elections for delegates to a convention that would draft a state constitution. The elections were organized by the Free State Executive Committee, a group of leading Kansas abolitionists. The committee considered the elections necessary because "our ballot boxes have been taken possession of by bands of armed men from foreign states" who elected a "so-called Legislature, unacquainted with our wants, and hostile to our best interests. . . ."

On October 9, 1855, the twenty-one-year-old Rufus Crosby of Oceana was elected to the Topeka Constitutional Convention. He was the youngest convention delegate as his twenty-first birthday came four days prior to the election; otherwise he would have been ineligible. The convention secretary—eyeing history—had each of the delegates sign his name and provide other pertinent information about himself. The secretary said he wanted history to show that not all of the convention delegates were "abolitionists from Boston, Massachusetts, hired to come to Kansas by the Emigrant Aid Society." When Rufus Crosby signed the document—"to be deposited . . . in the Archives of the State of Kansas for future Lithographing"—he supplied his name, residence, occupation, place of birth, age, marital status, and political party. The young delegate signed: "R.H. Crosby, Ocena, Merchant, Maine, 21, Single, Republican." The convention met from October 23 until November 11 at Convention Hall. Delegates, it was agreed,

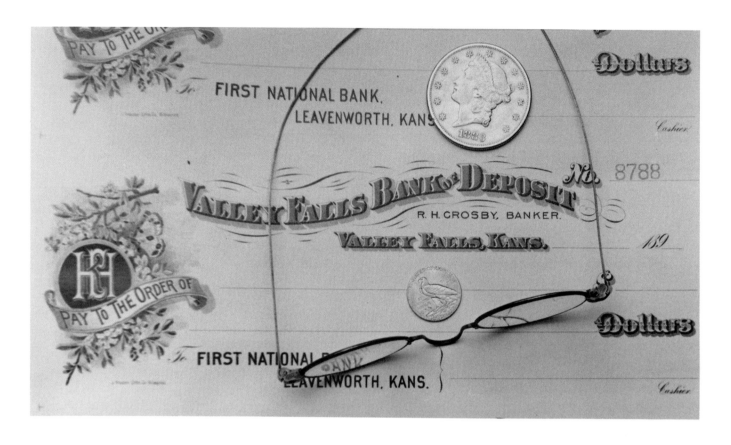

The stylized monogram of Rufus H. Crosby appeared on checks that were issued by his Valley Falls Bank of Deposit and cleared through the First National Bank of Leavenworth. Most transactions, however, were conducted with gold coins similar to these found in the old bank building.

would receive $3.00 a day and $3.00 for every twenty miles traveled to and from the convention. The costs of the convention came to $15,265.90. Invoice #9 was paid to R. H. Crosby in the amount of $108.00 for "services as member of Con.Convention."

The delegates approved a constitution, a state bill of rights, and two propositions that were to be presented to the voters for ratification on December 15. One proposition concerned a state banking law, and the other sought to exclude slavery from the state. The measures passed in lopsided voting. Favoring the constitution were 1,731 votes with 41 against, but the proslavery factions did not recognize the election. The new constitution seeking admission of Kansas into the Union as a free state was not accepted by Congress or by President Franklin Pierce. The struggle between the free-soil advocates and the proslavery factions continued until 1861 when Kansas joined the Union as a free state.

In the spring of 1856, the Crosby brothers moved thirty miles southwest of Oceana to start another dry-goods store in the Jefferson County town of Grasshopper Falls, the name of which would be changed to Valley Falls years later. Political tensions continued to heighten, and men on both sides of the controversy began arming themselves. The antagonism developed into a relentless guerrilla war between Free-Soilers and Border Ruffians throughout the summer of 1856. There were raids on Lawrence by proslavery forces and a brutal retaliation in Osawatomie, where five proslav-

ery men were murdered by John Brown and his band. The ongoing border war attracted national attention, which brought aid to both sides.

Rufus Crosby, a framer of a state constitution, now became Captain Crosby commanding the local free-soil militia, a company of twenty-five to thirty men. The company built a small fortification on the banks of the Delaware River and maintained a vigilant watch for movement by Border Ruffians who used Atchison and the surrounding countryside for their base. On September 12, a group of proslavery South Carolinians, known as the Palmetto Guard, attacked Grasshopper Falls. The proslavery newspaper, the *Sovereign Squatter*, published in Atchison, carried a detailed account of how "white-livered Yankees" ran when they heard the Border Ruffians' rebel yell:

> "At the time of the attack, Capt. Crosby's company numbering about thirty, were on parade, but scattered like a flock of startled sheep without firing a gun. So terror-stricken were they that numbers of them lay in corn fields and permitted our troops to pass within a short distance of them without firing a gun.
>
> "Crosby's store, with all its contents—consisting chiefly of provisions and supplies for the band of thieves whose rendezvous was at that point—was burned to the ground. Some arms and horses, stolen during the depredations of Crosby's gang, were brought away, but everything else that could be used to sustain the midnight assassins was destroyed."

After their store burned, Rufus secured a teaching position in Nodaway County in northwest Missouri and stayed for the winter term. William returned home to Maine. By the next spring, the two brothers were reunited and back in business in Grasshopper Falls. They rebuilt the store on the same lot. There were only six other buildings in the entire 320-acre town site: three houses, a blacksmith shop, a drug store, and the Cataract Hotel opposite the Crosby brothers' store. Building did pick up after the official land sales in August 1857, which finally gave property owners clear title to town lots where they intended to build. The Crosby brothers secured title to their property from the town company for $240 in September 1857, a year that saw the completion of another twelve buildings. Census takers that year counted 1,962 residents in the county, 60 of whom were slaves.

By the summer of 1858, it was evident that the town would survive. There were forty to fifty buildings, two saw mills, and a brick manufacturer. The town boasted five stores and its own newspaper in which "Crosby and Brother, General Merchandise Emporium" advertised its wares. Dry hot weather between 1854 and 1861, compounded by the political turmoil, resulted in extremely poor crops during the period. William and Rufus Crosby probably were helped through the hard times in 1860 by warranting sixty acres of farm land they owned outside of Grasshopper Falls to their father Samuel back in Maine for the sum of $1,500.

Earning a living was hard and almost anything was accepted as money. Hundreds of various bank notes were used as script. Some circulated on par value with gold, but most were discounted. The 1858 discovery of gold at Pike's Peak prompted a minor gold rush that allured many Kansas

"Times have been almost intolerably hard. Men can neither pay or get paid. By an unlimited system of mutual credit, all manage to obtain a bare subsistence without actual suffering and are content with that. There is little ambition & no business."

Rev. Oswald Woodford,
Congregationalist minister
Grasshopper Falls, 1858

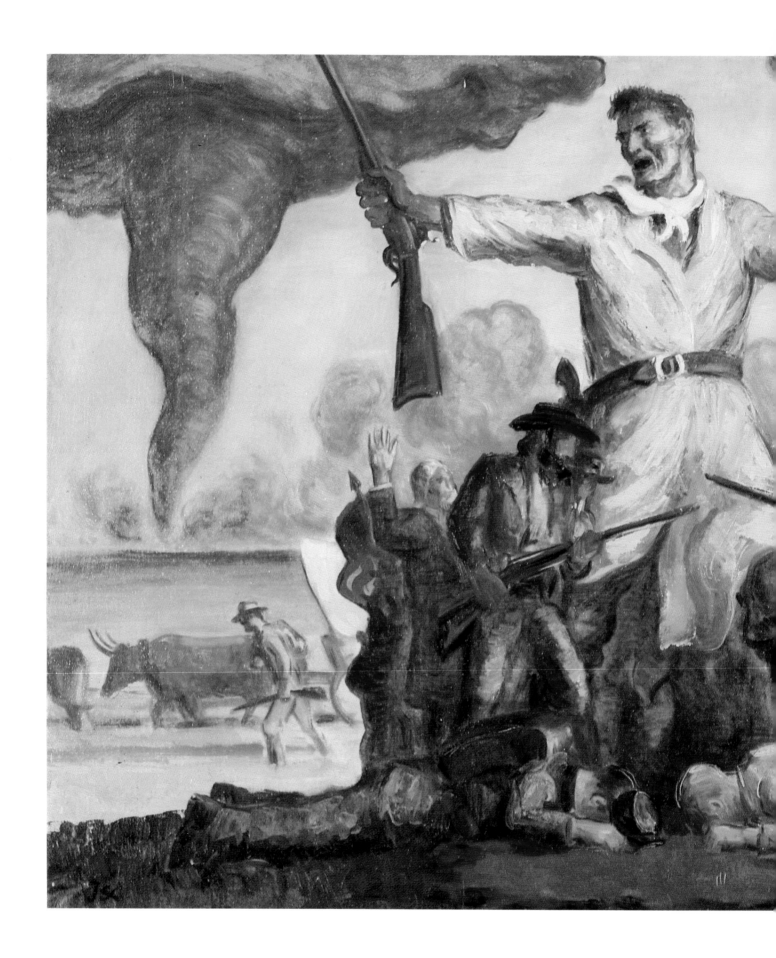

The Tragic Prelude, *(1938)*
oil, 30x45 in.,
John Steuart Curry

Nettie Crosby, about 1880

settlers to make the five-hundred-mile trip from Leavenworth to Colorado with a team of oxen. Crosby Brothers, in a June 1860 newspaper advertisement, showed their willingness to do business regardless of currency:

"**To Our Staunch and Thrifty Customers!** Who don't go to the Peak, and who have known us, many of them, since before the war, we would merely say that we have established the following as currency in exchange for goods, **Viz:** Gold (Pike's Peak or otherwise), Silver and Good Bank Bills, Coon Skins, Butter, Beef Hides, Cheese, Potatoes, Eggs, Brooms, Tallow, Pork, Mink and Otter Skins, Lard, Wheat, Oats, Peas, Beans, Barley, & c., in fact, anything most, but a **slow** note."

The retailers offered a $5,000 reward—their entire stock—to any Jefferson County merchant who could prove that he had sold more goods than the Crosby Brothers during the previous six months.

By this time, William Crosby had married; but his intense younger brother Rufus remained a bachelor until 1862. That spring Rufus returned home to Hampden, Maine, and there married Nettie Kendall on April 13 in the bride's home. The third of six children, Nettie also had grown up on a Hampden farmstead. After their marriage, the newlyweds traveled west to make their home in Grasshopper Falls, Kansas. Serious and severe, the newly married Rufus could not divorce himself from his political passions.

Rufus Crosby became editor of the Grasshopper Falls newspaper during the Civil War. The June 24, 1863, inaugural issue of the Kansas Jeffersonian *contained a personal column by the new editor, in which he expressed his passionate belief in the Union cause: "It is not strange that our Kansas boys have gained an immortal reputation as fighting men in this struggle, for they above all others, have a 'preemption right' to kill proslavery rebels."*

An 1863, he served briefly as editor for the town newspaper, which he named the *Kansas Jeffersonian*. An able and articulate writer, Rufus Crosby bitterly reflected for his readers his enduring hatred for supporters of slavery. "Seven years ago," he wrote in June 1863, "we saw the last dollar's worth of our property destroyed on this very spot by the minions of slavery, and as we beheld the flames towering aloft that we well knew were rendering us houseless and a beggar, we vowed that henceforth we would not rest satisfied, until the black, unscrupulous slave oligarchy were humbled." Rufus welcomed free black slaves into the community, writing in his newspaper: "Coming among us as they do when laborers are scarce, with such dispositions as they have shown, they cannot but be useful; and it only remains for our citizens to encourage them in their well doing—to allow them religious and educational privileges." On the town streets, Rufus practiced and drilled the Grasshopper Falls Militia Company that he had helped to organize following the bloody raid by William Quantrill on Lawrence, Kansas. William and Rufus spearheaded a drive to send money and flour to Lawrence; the brothers contributed $25, the largest amount.

The opinionated Rufus was an influential leader in the prairie community but was not always well liked. A. B. Patrick, editor of the *Oskaloosa Times*, had met Rufus in the spring of 1857 when he was rebuilding his burned-out store. Patrick, a friend and colleague, wrote candidly that Rufus Crosby was "intensely insolent and abusive" and "overbearing and discourteous in personal conversation" though possessing a "most kindly and forgiving disposition." Patrick continued, "[Rufus Crosby] was vindictive, and often flew to the prints to inflict punishment on some guilty head, and was at times seemingly cruel and unrelenting, yet not malicious, but for his

THE KANSAS JEFFERSONIAN.

R. H. CROSBY,] FIRST PURE, THEN PEACEABLE. [Editor and Proprietor.

VOL. I. GRASSHOPPER FALLS, JUNE 24, 1863. NO. I.

The Jeffersonian

Published every Wednesday at
GRASSHOPPER FALLS,
Jefferson County, Kansas.

R. H. Crosby, - Editor & Proprietor.
P. H. Peters, - - Publisher.

Terms of Subscription:

Single copy one year in advance -	$2.00
Ten copies one year to one address	15.00
Twenty " " " " "	25.00
Fifty " " " " "	50.00

Terms of Advertising:

One square, 10 lines or less, first insertion - - - -	$1.00
" " each additional "	50
" " two months,	2 50
" " three "	4 00
" " six "	6 00
" " twelve "	10 00
One quarter of a column three months - - -	10 00
" six "	15 00
" twelve "	25 00
Changeable quarterly	30 00
One half of a column three "	15 00
" six "	25 00
" twelve "	40 00
Changable quarterly	50 00
One column three months	30 00
" six "	45 00
" twelve "	60 00
Changeable quarterly	75 00

Editorial notices 20 cents per line; Local 15 cents. For announcing the names of candidates for office, one dollar and a half each, to be paid in advance. Yearly advertisers will be required to pay quarterly. Transient advertisements must be paid in advance. Communications of a personal character will be charged one dollar per square.

For yearly or semi-yearly advertisements, special contracts made.

All letters on business connected with this paper must be directed to
R. H. CROSBY,
Editor and Proprietor.

OUR COUNTRY'S CALL.

BY JOHN PIERPONT.

Air—"Scots Wha Hae," etc.

Men who plow your granite peaks,
O'er whose head your Eagle shrieks,
And for aye of Freedom speaks,
Hear your country's call!
Swear, each loyal mother's son,
Swear "Our country shall be One!"
Seize your sword, or bring your gun,
Bayonet and ball!

For the land that bore you—Arm!
Shield the State you love from harm!
Catch, and round you spread, the alarm;
Hear, and hold your breath!
Hark! the hostile horde is nigh!
See the storm comes roaring by!
Hear and heed our battle cry—
"Victory or Death!"

Sturdy landsmen, hearty tars,
Can you see your Stripes and Stars
Flouted by the three broad bars,
And cold-blooded feel?
There the rebel banner floats!
Tyrants vanquished by your votes,
Spring like bloodhounds, at your threats:
Let them bite your steel!

With no traitor at their head,
By no braggart coward led,
By no hero caught a-bed,
While he dream of flight;
By no "Young Napoleons,"
Kept at bay by wooden guns,
Shall our brothers and our sons,
Be held back from fight!

Like a whirlwind in its course,
Shall again a rebel force,
Jackson's foot or Stuart's horse,
Pass our sleepy posts?,
Roam, like Satan, "to and fro,"
And our Laggard let them go?
No! in thunder answer "No!
By the Lord of Hosts!"

With the Lord of Hosts we fight,
For his freedom, Law and Right—
Strike for these, and h's all-might
Sha'll with victory crown
Loyal brows, alive or dead,
Crush each crawling Copperhead,
And in bloody battle tread
This rebellion down!

Talk of "Peace" in hours like this?
'Tis Iscariot's traitor kiss,
'Tis the Old Serpent's latest hiss!
Foil his foul intrigue!
Plant your heel his head upon!
... is run!
Now to keep your Country one,
Join our Union League!

Fixing Sounds.—Some months ago, M. Scoot, well know among the savans of Paris, exhibited experements of a very interesting charater, in the art of fixing sounds. The same specie of natural means so successfully employed in photography with reference to form, namely, the aerial undulations of which sounds consist, are by the construc- of the *photograph*, made ingeniously to subserve the intricate purpose in view. The representation of the various curves and vibrations performed by an instrument of highly susceptible mobility, whilst acted upon by these atmospheric movements, has been perfectly accomplished and although a serious difficulty seems to obstruct the re translation of this somewhat indefinite language into the regulad and fixed signs for the verbal sounds which produced it, M. Scott is sufficiently sanguine about the result to give cause for alarm in the minds of the short-hand writer whose occupation would be more detrimentally affected by this wonderful apparatus for reporting than even that ot artists has been by the sister invention of photog aph.

Comfort at Home.—A powerful attraction to home is a cultivation of a spirit of neatness and elegance throughout all its arrangements. The eye scarcely ever wearies of a beautiful prospect or a pleasant picture. The aspect of a home should resemble the latter; it should tell its own tale; its atmosphere should breathe of comfort, and its quiet simple ornamentation delight the eye. There is a brightness about a well kept home, which neither wealth nor magnificence can impart, unaccompanied by taste. To keep best anything to be used only for visitors' accommodation, is not the wisest policy for a wife to adopt; on the contrary, company rooms contrast too greatly with daily living rooms, and suggest unpleasant comparisons. Neatness and elegance go hand in hand, one cannot exist without the other; but it must be neatness far removed from formality, and elegance independent of costliness and profusion. Every article should appear as though intended for use, and every article in its right place, the very chairs and tables should be suggestive of comfort; not arranged with stiff precision, but in such a way that the attractive portion of a room will be visible to its occupants.

Josh Billings on War Frazes.—"War ov exterminashun," this fraze belongs wholly to the Kommissary Department.
"Awl quiet on the Potomuck," this shows what perfect subjeckshun our feller air under.

☞ Virtue finds its securest home among the sons of poverty, as a delicate flower is safest from violation when shut in by the unsightly and rugged rocks.

Sol Miller says that Stonewall Jackson was a religious cuss.

ONE OF MANY.

Oh! how the music, the wild war-music rose and swelled as the company marched down the street of the little country town! How the banners shook and bayonets glitterd in the August sunshine! Blue were the skies over-head, and along the wayside the fields were green, and the scent of flowers was in the air. For a moment Margery Dane looked out from her window; then she drew down the curtain, and held her hands over her ears, trying to shut out sight and sound.

"Are they treading on the ground or on my heart?" she cried, with a passionate despair in her tones. "He is marching away, and he will never march back again. Pity me, Heaven; I am losing my last sight at him."

Up again went the curtain, but the last man had gone by. The martial music floated back, softened by distance to pity and tender pain, instead of triumph. Margery was indeed alone.

She had had a lonely life. Not that she had been poor, or ill-treated, or in any wise persecuted. But she had neither father nor mother brother nor sister. She had a fortune of her own; a very comfortable one they called it in that little country town; and the uncle and aunt with whom she lived were kind to her and seldom crossed her wishes. But if you have ever lived just such a life, you know what loneliness means. One would rather have even harsh blame from those whose love is their authority then the cool kindness of people too indifferent to censure. Margery had not been morbid or sentimental in girlhood, or even childhood. When her heart ached for love, for mother-kisses and fatherly praises, she scarcely understood what she wanted herself and only betrayed the secret pain by her utter recklessness of danger. No boy in Westville rode such gay horses, or climbed such high trees, because not a boy there but knew some heart would ache if it befell him. Want of love made Margery reckless.

But when she was sixteen love came. It was the old, sweet story. She grew in six months from romping, reckless girlhood to gentle, reticent, and most graceful womanhood All the tenderness of her nature, which had waited so many years for its object, overflowed at last: longing, dreaming heart, passionate, earnest soul were satisfied. And for once she built no alter to a false idol. Her nature was so pure it tested those she met like a touchstone It had no affinity with evil, and her choice fell worthily. Nelson Hardy dserved all—love, confidence, tender girlish trust. I think, too, his devotion was not less intense than her own—not less utterly absorbing. He too, was an orphan, and the new tie was his all.

They had been engaged six months when the war broke out. They were not to marry for two or three years; but they met daily, and so waiting was not wearisome. When the war began Margery had been half afraid Nelson would think that his duty called him; but he told her he would wait untill there was need of him—so many were ready to go then. So she had a year and over to be happy in. Then came the call for three hundred thousand, and two three nights afterward Nelson Harding, with the words she dreaded—

"I ought to go, Margery. Shall I?"

"Go home now, Nelson, and come and ask me again to-morrow.

She dared not answer him then, for she was torn between the fear of losing him and the fear of doing wrong. She felt that She must be alone in the universe with God in order to the truth clearly.

When he was gone she went up stairs to the little room where, for so many years, the solitary child had cried out of her heart; else muttered loneliness to the "solitary God." What was required of her now? When Heavens gave her no father or mother, only Nelson, was it not meant that she should keep the gift? Could it be that already the giver was asking for it back again? And yet were not the chosen people in all ages taught to offer of their best—to lay their first fruits upon the altar? Ought she not to think it Heaven's bounty that gave her opportunity to make a sacrifice so costly?

All the night she sat there before her window, or knelt beside her bed, untill the daily miracle of dawning repeated itself—repeated its tender pink flushes above the hills, its tremulous mists, its air of balm, its broadening glory of sunrise! Soon he would come. Soon she must tell him what to choose; life and love for her and him, or—the right. With that word her soul grew strong She would be the consolor, not the temptress.

When her lover looked into her eye he knew her thought. Still he asked the question,

"What am I to do, Margery?"

"What God and your own soul tell you?"

"And you, child?"

"I am to wait and bear; or, perhaps, I too shall find my work."

So Nelson Harding had marched away in the August sunshine, and Margery Dane was to commence her waiting.

Honor to the brave who fight and conquer, or fight and fall! But is theirs the hardest fate? Do not those suffer more who can not lose in action their fear and anguish? who must count slow hours, shudder at tidings of onward movements, live on fragments of newspapers? Ay; and is it not true that every bullet shoots double and the shot which flies farthest makes the sorest wound?

But Margery's waiting did not last long. So soon, that it scarcely seemed as if the regiment could have reached its destination, the news of Antetiam came. The Sixteenth were engaged in it, and she read among the wounded the name, Lieutenant Nelson Harding. She was a slight, tdelicately-organized little thing. Her tall, strong lover had been wont to call her child but the child did not shriek or faint. She did not even cry. Some spirit other than her own seemed to have taken possession of her—a cool, brave spirit, strong to do and to dare! She went to the room where her uncle and aunt were sitting together. They started when they saw the white, firm face, whence all the pink prettiness was gone as utterly as if it had been touched by death.

"I am going to Washington, uncle. Lieutenant Harding's wounded. He will be in the hospital. The next train leaves in an hour."

"But child, you must ... alone!" said Mr. Dane, with ... face and wondering eyes. "Do you want me?"

"As you please. It might be a help, if you could get away in time. There is only an hour."

She shut the door. Her uncle and aunt exchanged glances.

"She will go," Mrs. Dane said; "I know her. Of course, you had better go to take care of her."

That settled it. Mrs. Dane's judgement were always final.

When the long journey was over, and Mr. Dane and his niece stood on the the threshold of the Baltimore hospital, to which they had been sent from Washington, they met there a Connecticut surgeon whom they knew. Mr. Dane inquired of him for Lieutenant Hardsng.

"There is no hope for him, poor fellow!" was the answer, and then Surgeon Hunt met Margery's eyes, and remembered that she was Nelson Hading's promised wife. He murmured a sincere but half indistinct apology, which her clear tones cut short:

"Thank you—do not blame yourself. I wanted to hear the truth. It was best that I should know it before I saw him. Now show me where he is, please."

"Nelson!"

She had been standing for a moment watching him. Eyes and mouth were shut resolutely against tear or moan. But his ghastly face was eloquent. She could see in his convulsed features the tortures he was bearing silently. At her voice his eyes opened. The old fond look replaced the pain in them. I think he forgot for a moment that he was suffering when he saw the slight form at his bedside, and heard the voice, the well loved voice. He put out his hand:

"Child—love—Margery!"

"Did you expect me, Nelson?"

"To-morrow, not to-day. I had not thought you could be here so soon. I was waiting for your coming to die I think I should have waited a week if need were. But the agony is horrible."

She bent over him, and left a kiss on the pale forehead. He drew her closer then, and his lips clung to hers with a long, despairing pressure.

"To think after to-night I shall never kiss you again, Margery. If we meet in heaven it will not be as here. I shall love your spirit; but it seems to me I shall miss all this vanished sweetness of tender eyes, loveing lips, softly falling hair. God help us, child how little the best of us know where we are going!"

Then she comforted him with her cleaevr vision, her stronger faith. It could not be for long, she whispered, their parting. She would be his, through all eternity, just as truly as now.

For hours he lay with her in his—waiting. It was a strange feeling he had had when he heard her voice and met her eyes—a feeling that she had brought him his release from pain—that now even Death would treat him gently. But the strange thought may have been true. Through those long waiting hours with her hand in his, he did not suffer. He only felt his strength ebbing away, and knew that his life was dissolving into moments. Just at the last his face brightennd, and he whispered.

"Something tells me you are right Margery. The future will not be dim and pale besid the present it will be brighter. My soul before it leaves the body is asserting its own immortality. I know now that I shall live hereafter. Never think you are solitary again, child. I shall live, and I shall love you. Day-times and night-tides will bring you nearer to me, each one."

Then a pause, broken only by her tears, which wet his hair, and her kisses on his lips—then he cried, with one last effort,

"Never be sorry Margery, that I went. I am not. I fell doing God's work. If I had turned my back upon the right I should have lost more than life. God loves you. Margery. Be patient. One more kiss."

She bent to give it to him, but when she raised her head there was no light in the swiftly glazing eyes—his soul was marching on.

Oh, If I could but have told that he got better—that her coming brought him healing—that he lived to love her in this world! You would not have thought my story so sad then; but mayhap it would have been sadder. It is the sleep which knows no earthly waking, ... not the life of earth which God promises as a reward to His beloved and is there not something at once nobler and more joyful than life in dying for a good cause? The story of such a death should kindle courage. There are still souls left strong enough to give thanks for martyrdom.

Margery Dane found her work when Nelson Harding died. She is a nurse in a hospital—so grave, so still, so thoughtful, and so tender, that her youth is pardoned and forgotten, even as she has forgotten it herself. I think she will live while her country has need of her, and then she will not be sorry to go to her love and her rest.

A correspondent thus describes the weather in Arkansas:

After a hard day's ride, we have returned nearly dead with fatigue—without an appetite—glad to rest even on a dry board. At such times, how the home of childhood looms up! The water here seems soft and slippery, as if it had been greased with old lard, or last year's goose oil. It is wet, but a gallon of it will not quench thirst. A man's mouth tastes as though he had been chewing old tobacco quids picked from hotel spittoons His flesh feels hot and rough. The air seems to stick to his lungs like a wet shirt to the back, giving no actual life. Food tastes diferent—like unchafed grain going through a fanning mill. A man's stomach feels within him like a scared cat just ready to jump through the window, while his bowels feel like a brass band tuning up after a long vacation.—We have not aimed to be funny in this description, only to give the actual state of the way a Northern man feels in this atmosphere, whose rider is death.

Beecher says: "The devil does not trap twice alike. If yesterday he came through vanity, to-day he will come through pride. If to-day he comes on one side, to-morrow he will come on another. And we are always watching for him at the hole he came in last; while he is digging a new one."

True courage always counts the peril as an agile leap is always measured firs. with a cool, clear eye.

☞ The soldiers in the vicinity of Corinth, Miss., are marrying the females thereabouts, with the limitation added to the contract, "while the war lasts."

A Scotch Anecdote.—A Scotch parson in his prayer said, "Laird bless the grand council and parliment and grant they hang together." A country fellow standing by replied. "Yes, yes, with all my heart, a d the sooner, the better, and I am sure it is the prayer of all good people." "But, friends," said the parson, "I don't mean as that fellow does, but pray that they may hang together in accord concord" No matter what cord," replied the other "so that it is a *strong cord.*"

There is a town in Maine called Random. A resident of the place being asked where he lived, said he lived at *Random.* He was taken up as a vagrant.

Sol. Miller's Idea of Hell.

We wish some genius orthodox, who has made the subject his study and professes to understand it, would inform us what is the use of a Hell? We have never been a church member and have not investigated such matters very deeply; but we have always been a firm believer in a Hell—a little place of burning and howling, as described in Holy Writ. We took a secret pleasure in the thought that there was such a place, for the benfit of villains whose cases could not be sufficiently reached by all the punishment and torture that could be inflicted in this world. In our younger days, we imagined the place was reserved exclusively for Democrats, especialy those who did not vote for Henry Clay for President. Then, as we grew older, and listened to the arguments of "Universalians,' and other anti-hellions, we began to think it might not be so bad, after all. In fact, we don't know what to believe about, it and regretted that there was any room for doubt; for it was like waking out of a pleasent dream. But every calamnity, brings some useful lesson; and when this rebellion broke out, amid our sorrow for the ruin and desolation which it would produce, we had one ray of pleasure. It firmly re-established our belief in a regular, good old, old-fashioned, Hard-Shell Baptist Hell, where the images get up and yelp, and the devil, with horns in his head, and a spear on the end of his tail, and cloven feet, piles the hot brimstone around them with a big hook—such a place as John Calvin endeavored to convince Michael Servetus of the existence, by giving him a slight touch of quality. Having confessed our faith, and giving our idea of the character and use of the institu- we would now be pleased if Henry Ward Beecher, or some other fire and brimstone champion, would tell us what a Hell is for. The present rebellion is the greatest and most unpardonable crime that has been committed since the rebellion in Heaven; yet, when prime movers and master-spirits in this crime meet their just fate—meet it in the very act of murdering the nation and its defenders—their virtues and Christianity are extolled by such men as Beecher, and they are straightway given a pass to Heaven. There never was barbarians or cannibals so brutal and devlish as the Southern rebels, yet Northern men are constantly endeavoring to smuggle them into Paradise. Stonewall Jackson, Zollicoffer, and even Ben. McCullough have been sent up there and Gen. Lee has all his papers made out in regular style, ready to start upon short notice. Then, what is Hell for? If Southern and Northern traitors do not go there, nobody else will, and there is a famous institution, with fires in every room, to let cheap. For particulars enquire at the premises

A Good Shot.—I never pass the old toll gate at Newcastle bridge without thinking of George Schaffer, who many years ago lived in Portsmouth. I must tell it as a tribute to his memory. Once he had been in Newcastle, gunning, and was coming home with his game bag empty, and was very weary, when he stopped at the toll-house for a moment's rest. Says he to the toll-taker, 'There's a fine flock of ducks back here in the pond; what will you let me fire into them for?' 'Can't do it,' replied the toll-man 'I don't want to have my ducks killed.' George put his gun into the toll-house, and walked back to take another look at the ducks. While he was gone, the toll-man, who was a wag drew the shot from the barrel and then replaced the gun. George returned and renewed the question. 'Well,' said the toll-man though you are called a good shot, I don't believe you can hurt them much, Give me a dollar and you may fire. The dollar was paid; quite a party who had gathered round, went back to witness Gorge's discomforture. He raised his gun, fired and killed nine of them. 'The devil!' cried the toll-man in consternation, 'how did you do that I took the charge out of your gun.' 'Yes,' said George, 'I supposed you would. I always go double charged.

—*B. P Shillaber.*

Dr. Adam Clark—Had a perfect abhorrence of both pork and tobacco. He is reported to have said: "If I were to offer a sacrifice to the Devil, it would be a roasted pig stuffed with tobacco."

What three words did Adam use when he introduced himself to Eve and which read the same backward and forward? "Madam, I'm Adam."

THE FARMERS' COLUMN.

Farmers' Boys.—In the world there is no mor important thing than farmers' boys. They are not so important now as they will be. At present they are of little consequence too often. But farmers boys always have been, and we presume always will be, the material out of which the noblest men are made. They have health and strength; they have bone and muscle; they have heart and will; they have ambition and endurance, and there are the materials that make men. Not buckram and broadcloth, and patent leather and beaver fur, and kid gloves and watch-seals, are the materials of which men are made. It is not fat and flesh, and swagger and self-conceit, nor yet smartness, nor flippancy, nor foppery, nor fastness. These make fools, not men; not men such as the world want, nor such as it will honor and bless. Not long hair, not much beard, nor a cane, nor a pipe, nor segar, nor quid of tobacco, nor an oath, nor a glass of beer or brandy, nor a dog or gun, nor a pack of cards, nor a novel, nor a vulgar book of love and murder, a tale of adventures, that make a man, or has anything to do with making a man. Farmer's boys ought to keep clear of all these idle, foolish things. They should be employed with nobler objects. They should be men of clear grit—honest intelligent, industrious men. —*Valley Spirit.*

The Profits Of Fruit Growing.—There is no question but fruit growing has been a source of great profit to farmers of Western New York within the last fifteen years. and, strange as it may seem, the business improves as the number of growers increases.

An instance of the advantage of fruit growing is related by the Orleans *American.* A lady in the town Gaines bought, eight years ago eight acres of old, worn-out land, at less than $40 per acre; cropped it two years, ... years last November) set it out to orchard at an expense of less than $200, over and above expenses. She recently declined an offer of $2,500 for the field—will not sell for less than $3,000. There is no building or other imprevement on the land except those mentioned, —[*Rochester Union and Adv.*

Mutton vs. Pork —Physicians recommend mutton as the most wholesomse meat—the easiest digested, and the best suited to invalids, while pork, as everybody knows, is the most unwholesome flesh eaten. In England mutton is a favorite dish, and we apprehend that it is to this more than to roast beef, that the Englishman owes his robust health and rosy complexion.

Our people eat too much pork and not enough mutton, and yet, as a cotemporary well remarks, "mutton can be produced pound for pound at less than half the price of pork; yields more nourishment when eaten, and keeping sheep does not exhaust a farm to the extent feeding hogs does. Sheep can be kept during the winter on hay or turnips, or mangel wurtzel, or sugar beet, while hogs will not do without at least some corn." We would like to see in the papers fewer accounts of big pigs, and more fat sheep.

Care of Sheep.—It is proved beyond controversy that wool, with proper care of the sheep, will improve year to year, both in quantity and quality; but care must be taken. A friend just came in and said, "Another sheep gone. This makes three out of eleven." And I might add the other eight are ready to follow. And all this for want of attention. The sheep were sheared, and put out to pasture on a bleak hill, without protection. A cold rain ensued which lasted for days. The sheep were chilled; cold and death ensued—for a sheep, like any other animal, is subject to taking cold. This must be guarded against. A humane man, if he is also intelligent, and has withal an eye to the pocket, will see that not only suffering is avoided, but all danger. He will see that his naked sheep are sheltered, as you, as everybody, would want to be. Suffering of any kind will always hurt a sheep—will hurt its quality of wool, and its quantity: two important things to the wool-grower.—*Valley Farmer.*

Let your domstic animals have salt.

A wealthy Frenchman, in Naples, recently committed suicide by cutting off his head with a gullotine of his own contrivance, which he had erected in his own apartments. He was neatly beheaded, and his head in a basket.

Alvin D. Kendall, 1919

In 1877, Rufus Crosby and Alvin Kendall moved their dry-goods store from the corner of Sycamore and Louisa streets to a new building on Broadway, which had become the main street in Valley Falls, Kansas. When Rufus Crosby went into banking in 1879, Kendall became the sole proprietor and dropped Crosby from the store name. The second floor of the building was used for Masonic meetings, plays, and other community activities.

In August of 1874, grasshoppers were seen on the horizon days in advance like a coming snowstorm, but nothing could be done to halt the approaching swarms. They ate all the growing crops, laid their eggs, and then died, filling the air with a sordid stench. So many grasshoppers were squashed on the railroad tracks near Topeka, Kansas, that the rails became extremely slick; and the Union Pacific trains were stalled because of a lack of traction.

life couldn't help manifesting his fighting stock, often officiously inter-meddling improperly. But he couldn't help it."

Much of Patrick's harsher criticisms related to Rufus Crosby's public efforts to rid his town of liquor. For Rufus Crosby, slavery was not the only evil that darkened the hearts of men. Liquor came a close second. "We consider the liquor business the greatest curse a country ever had," Rufus wrote in 1863. "Scarcely a hamlet on our western frontier but contains a licensed or an unlicensed doggery dealing out death and damnation to its victims." Rufus and William Crosby each contributed $50 to the "Ladies Temperance Vigilance Committee" for "redeeming the City of Grasshopper Falls—and keeping it perpetually so redeemed—from the curse of Rum traffic." Rufus saw the temperance effort as divinely inspired. "I recognize no head to this spontaneous Temperance uprising other than God himself and believe that it is His Spirit, working on the consciousness of most all of us, to raise our arm to stay the awful curse of rum traffic," he said.

In August 1874, hordes of grasshoppers swarmed over Kansas destroying crops just as the heads of wheat were ready to harvest. To be ingloriously named for the despised grasshopper was a decided embarrassment for the town. Other Kansas towns had chosen the names of early settlers, presidents, Indians, or ideals, such as the towns named Independence or Enterprise. But Rufus Crosby's community had chosen an insect for its name, a reviled insect at that. The next year, the city of Grasshopper Falls successfully petitioned the state legislature for approval to change the name of the town to Valley Falls.

Despite the hard times, Rufus and Nettie Crosby had prospered. Farmers might have a bad year; but they still needed the notions, sugar, flour, clothes, and coffee that were available at the Crosbys' dry-goods store. Rufus gave Nettie's brother Alvin Kendall a working interest in the store; and in 1868, Kendall bought out William Crosby. The store name was changed to Crosby and Kendall. When the census taker came around in 1869, the thirty-five-year-old Rufus Crosby shared a household with his twenty-eight-year-old wife and three-year-old daughter Charlotte. He listed his occupation as merchant and farmer and valued his real estate at $12,000 with another $10,000 of personal property. Rufus knew how to handle money; consequently, it was not surprising in 1879 when the merchant stepped forward to announce his intentions of starting his own bank after Hillyer and the Valley Bank and Savings Institution had gotten into trouble.

There was nothing fancy about the old bank building that Rufus Crosby took over when he bought the goodwill of the failed Valley Bank and Savings Institution. Rufus had plans for his Valley Falls Bank of Deposit. The bank was growing; and in February 1880, a land department was formed at the rear of the bank. Other employees were added, including the banker's wife Nettie who became cashier. Initially, the bank had shared space with a dry-goods store, but by 1882 the bank required the whole lower floor of the building for its commercial operations. If Rufus took personal responsibility for the bank's deposits, he equally took credit for the institu-

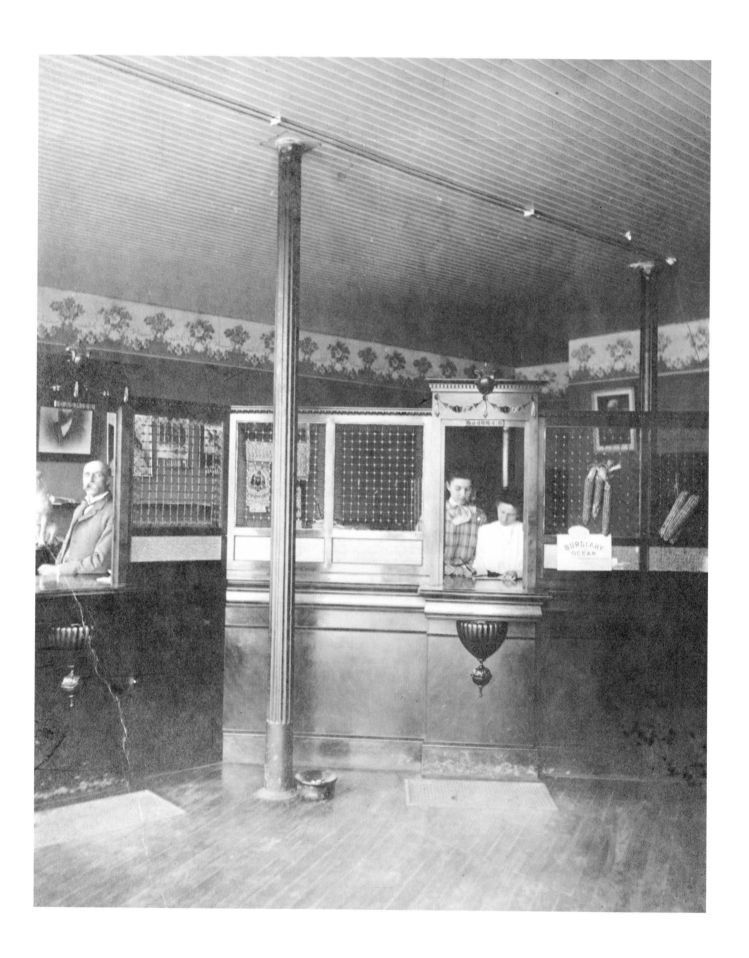

tion's success. The door of the vault plainly read: "R. H. Crosby's Valley Falls Bank of Deposit." The bank checks featured his stylized monogram.

Rufus considered applying for a national charter for his private bank, though he eventually decided against the change. "For six years we have had pigeonholed in our vault a full set of government papers to convert our bank into the First National Bank of Valley Falls, but on fuller examination found our present plan the best," he said. "Our business is run on the safe, sure and solid basis of economy. We have made a vow, and hope to have sufficient grit, gumption, and grace to fulfill it: Never during banking hours shall the doors of my bank be closed against the depositors." The bank's original capital of $50,000, the newspaper announced, had been doubled to $100,000 at the end of the bank's first six years in 1885.

*T*he Kansas Bankers Association—the nation's fourth oldest statewide banking association—was formed in Topeka in February 1887. Rufus Crosby was one of the sixty charter members and served for several years as the organization's first vice-president. Despite depressions and financial panics, the number of banks had grown tremendously in Kansas. The reasons were many: new towns were being started in the western regions; older communities were growing; currency was replacing barter as the medium of exchange; and, most importantly, starting a bank was easy.

Prior to 1891, the state had no banking regulations. That year the legislature passed a law that required five or more people to organize a bank, established a minimum capital of $5,000, and created the position of state banking commissioner. "For thirty years (prior) anyone who wanted to do so could open a bank, anywhere at any time," banking historian George Anderson explains. "A few dollars and a safe were all that he needed."

Rufus Crosby was fiscally conservative, not only in safeguarding his depositors' monies but also with the public purse. The opinionated banker was elected mayor of Valley Falls in 1887 and staunchly opposed the approval and issuance of several city bond issues. Rufus complained that the bonds had been privately placed without bids from two Valley Falls banks.

The ex-mayor gave a speech in March 1890 that he titled "How to Improve Valley Falls Financially." In it, Rufus Crosby bemoaned the fact that the city had more than $100,000 in outstanding bonds for railroads, schools, city water, and coal on which the city paid interest of $6,500 annually. The town, he said, was plagued by "peddling swindlers" and "patent right fiends." His bank, for one, had "proclaimed war on all these tall-hatted, well-dressed and slick-talking robbers" proposing deals around town. The banker said the town's prospects were bright. It had water power for mills, service by three railroads, and was developing some industries. "Financially, the darkest days for Valleys Falls are over," the banker concluded. ". . . The depression following the fool boom is nearly over."

That is what a young, ambitious, outgoing Missourian counted on when he decided to invest his savings in another Valley Falls dry-goods store. The youth had as much "grit, gumption, and grace" as his local banker. The young man, William Thornton Kemper, was not one to fail.

Alvin D. Kendall, brother-in-law of Rufus Crosby, poses with bank employees Roberta Zimmerman and Lida Goodrich in the lobby of the Valley Falls Bank of Deposit. Kendall bought the private bank in 1892 following the death of Rufus Crosby and changed the name to Kendall State Bank after obtaining a state charter in 1900. William T. Kemper worked as a teller in this bank.

GOING INTO BUSINESS

The Atchison, Topeka and Santa Fe Railway train eased out of the Saint Joseph railroad yard, slowly picking up steam. William Kemper, like any good salesman, knew all the little towns along the route, the first names of his customers, and his products—boots, shoes, and rubber goods. The twenty-year-old salesman for Noyes, Norman and Company, a Saint Joseph shoe distributor and manufacturer, had traveled eastern Kansas for over two years pursuing his boyhood ambition to be a wholesale shoe dealer and manufacturer. Now he was preparing to quit the train travel, the sales calls, and the nights and days away from home in favor of going into the retail business in Valley Falls, Kansas.

The Valley Falls newspaper announced Kemper's new enterprise in November 1885: "Walter Evans, well and favorably known to everybody in this city, and Wm. Kemper, the son of a successful wholesale dry-goods merchant, of St. Joe., Mo., have purchased Eli Evans's stock of goods and will take possession the first of January." The sales bills boldly stated: "Evans & Kemper, Dealers in Dry Goods, Boots, Shoes, Hats, Caps." Kemper, in later years, said he paid $2,000 to become the junior partner in the firm.

Moving to Valley Falls from Saint Joseph, Missouri, involved some major changes for William Kemper. Saint Joseph was a major wholesale center that boasted a population of 32,432 in 1880. The total population of Valley Falls was less than the largest church parish in Saint Joseph, where William Kemper's father James Madison Kemper had worked in retail trade.

Like so many other Missouri settlers, James Kemper was the child of a Kentucky farmer. He had visited his uncle J. Quincy Kemper in northern Missouri when he was seventeen years old and had decided to stay after he had secured a job at a general store in the tiny Missouri town of Mirabile. A handsome man, James Kemper became friends with the sons and daughter of James and Mary Paxton, another Kentucky family that had moved to Mirabile around 1850. In 1862, Kemper married Sallie Ann Paxton. The young couple moved to Hamilton, Missouri, during the Civil War. James, true to his origins, was a Confederate and was often called "Captain" Kemper by his friends.

On November 3, 1865, James and Sallie Ann Kemper became the

William T. Kemper, about 1880

Beef and Bread, *(1963)*
oil, 23½x29 in.,
Otto Kuhler

21

parents of a second child, their first son, whom they named William Thornton. The child was born in Gallatin, where the Kempers had moved. After his wife Sallie died, James Kemper moved to Saint Joseph and left William and his sister Jennie to live with Paxton relatives until they were able to join their father. In 1877, the eleven-year-old William got a job with the J. W. Bailey Dry Goods Company in Saint Joseph. When he was fourteen, William got a job with Collins and White, a shoe store in downtown Saint Joseph, and started out at $3 a week. William stood across the street from a downtown bank and wondered what he should do with his hard-earned money. "My friend Charles Enright, who was a clerk at the bank, stood there with me looking at the money. After a minute, Charley said, 'What are you going to do with it, Will?' And I said, 'I'm going to put part of it away.'"

That evening the boy and his father discussed business. It was a conversation the boy vividly remembered nearly fifty years later. His father, puffing on a pipe, took his son out to the porch where they talked about William's future in business. Kemper recalled the conversation this way: "Now, my son, are you sure you want to be a business man?" James Kemper asked. "Yes sir," the boy replied. His father continued, "Then this is my only advice to you: work at anything and save until you get enough money together to start a business of your own. Then go into business for yourself—if it is only a peanut stand. Without experience in business you may fail. But that is no disgrace, provided you take your shirt off your back to pay your creditors. The important thing is to strike out for yourself."

Three months after Kemper and Walter Evans took possession of the dry-goods store in 1886, the newspaper editor penned a short essay on the quality and character of Valley Falls and its residents. "Valley Falls needs no description," the editor wrote, then proceeded at great length to talk about the town:

"[The editor] knows its pleasant places, its genial society, its flourishing mercantile institutions, and the refining influence of its schools and churches. To the eye of the stranger, it is a picture, with its well kept lawns, wide streets, and the fine and comfortable homes, while here and there stand the sentinel churches. The population of our city is principally composed of the most substantial class of people, full of business, backbone and energy. . . . To those seeking a location for the investment and capital in a commercial way, the city of Valley Falls stands with a generous hand and welcoming arms extending to all who choose to take advantage of her facilities and make themselves fortunes, name, and fame within her borders."

Similar sentiments and hopeful prospects may have motivated William Kemper to move to Valley Falls, or it may have been the encouragement of his uncle Tom Paxton to take a financial interest in a dry-goods store in which Paxton had been an earlier partner. Initially, his investment in the store was intended to be more of a business opportunity than a decisive career change as Kemper continued to travel occasionally for Noyes, Norman and Company. He quickly made a name for himself and a favorable im-

Charlotte (Lottie) Crosby Kemper had considerable personal resources that had been left to her by her parents. William Kemper once suggested that she invest her money in The Kemper Investment Trust so that their sons could inherit the money. She responded, "My father told me always to keep my assets to myself."

Vassar College owed its existence largely to the personal fortune of Englishman Matthew Vassar, who had made a considerable fortune through brewing. He had endowed the college heavily and desired that "all sectarian influences should be carefully excluded" from the school curriculum. At that time, only the well-to-do were able to justify the expense and the advantages gained by higher education.

pression in the town. Among those most impressed with the salesman's business sense was the city's leading banker, Rufus Crosby.

In 1887, Rufus Crosby invited the twenty-one-year-old Kemper to become the bank's assistant cashier. Kemper accepted and two months later replaced the regular cashier, but he continued to maintain his interest in the dry-goods firm. The young man also was developing a growing interest in the banker's daughter Charlotte, whom he first met when Crosby invited William Kemper, the shoe salesman, to dinner. Known as Lottie, Charlotte had soft gentle eyes, a sweet smile, and a strong will. Her opinionated father and her education probably were equally responsible for the last quality.

Rufus and Nettie Crosby had made certain that their daughter received an excellent education. They sent Lottie forty miles away to Topeka to the College of Sisters of Bethany. The school, known for its strong art and music program, educated girls from kindergarten through college level. Her parents wanted an even better education for Lottie; so she traded an education on the plains of Kansas for schooling at Vassar College in Poughkeepsie, New York, a very proper school for well-to-do young women. Lottie attended the college's School of Music and Painting for the 1887–88 academic year. Vassar believed that "art stood boldly forth as an educating force, to have its fair play in the history of education." The year at Vassar fostered a great love for art in Lottie, which she enthusiastically and infectiously shared in later years with her own children and grandchildren.

Lottie shone in ways other than having a bright mind. Lottie performed in community plays, played the piano and organ, and was perhaps the most promising and eligible young woman in town. It is easy to understand—considering her education, artistic interests, and community standing—why Lottie's parents were a little perturbed when their daughter showed a great deal of interest in William Kemper, merchant and shoe salesman. Kemper liked beer and baseball and had not completed high school, but parents' opinions cannot rule a daughter's desires. The couple agreed to marry, her parents' objections notwithstanding. On June 10, 1890, William Thornton Kemper—son of Captain James Kemper, supporter of the South—married Charlotte Crosby—daughter of Captain Rufus Crosby, northern abolitionist. These two young adults, whose own parents had been on separate sides of a nation divided by the Civil War, united to form their own household. Kemper owned a dry-goods store; and shortly after their wedding, Lottie became organist for the Congregational Church. Six months prior to his marriage, Kemper had bought out the holdings of his business partner, Walter Evans, including the merchant's house. He then sold an interest in the dry-goods store to Daniel P. Paxton, a relative of his mother.

Kemper and Paxton were aggressive retailers. Kemper had an instinct and an ability for converting other people's business failures into his own successes. When a dry-goods store went bankrupt in the county seat of Oskaloosa, Kemper was there buying up the merchandise at "less than 50 cents on the dollar," which, he told the newspaper, "enabled [him] to give his customers unheard-of prices."

Nettie Crosby had worked as cashier in her husband's Valley Falls bank. Even after Rufus Crosby died in 1891, Nettie continued to make loans from money she kept stashed under her second-floor bed. A favorite family story tells how Grandmother Crosby guarded "the bank" by brandishing a shotgun and running off an intruder who was trying to break into her large, two-story home in Valley Falls, Kansas.

"The Kansas City of 1891 . . . was an overgrown city of a hundred thousand people. It was consciously citified, like a country jake in his first store clothes. . . . Its business area comprised of a dozen blocks in something like the center of town. To the west . . . were the packing houses. . . . Around them were the small industries of the city and the stockyards, which smelled to high heaven. . . . North of the business district was the red-light area, segregated and properly policed. South of the business area lived the ruling class in lovely homes. . . ."

William Allen White
Autobiography, 1946

In September 1891, after having controlled and operated his own bank for twelve years, Rufus invited his son-in-law to become a partner in the bank; and Kemper accepted. In the preceding year, Kemper had acquired a handsome home, a loving wife, and had just become a partner in a well-established bank. The twenty-five-year-old Kemper reasoned that if he could prove himself, eventually he could take over the bank if he adhered to the strict banking principles established by his father-in-law.

Three months later, Rufus Crosby was dead at the age of fifty-seven. For several days in late December 1891, the banker was nervous, complained of severe headaches, and seemingly was in failing health. On December 29, his wife found Crosby dead in the barn on the family farm. Within the week, the family discussed what to do with the bank. Alvin Kendall, the forty-six-year-old brother of Nettie Kendall Crosby, was to take over the bank from his deceased brother-in-law. The contract to sell the bank, dated January 7, 1892, was between Kendall and his sister Nettie Kendall Crosby and her daughter Charlotte Crosby Kemper. The terms called for Kendall to pay $400 the first year to rent the building and fixtures with an option to buy them for $4,000. Kendall assumed all of the bank's liabilities and was given the bank's reserve funds to cover the liabilities.

With Kendall running the bank, William Kemper began to rethink his own future. He and his wife had become the parents of a son, born on February 23, 1892, and had named him Rufus Crosby Kemper. The name was a verbal birthright to the first child born out of the union of the Crosby and Kemper families. The Kempers were anxious to leave Valley Falls; and by August 1892, Kemper had sold his interest in the store to his uncle Thomas Paxton, who immediately changed the name of the store to Paxton and Paxton. Preparing to move out of town, Kemper took out a notice in the October 1892 issue of the newspaper: "Having sold my business to Paxton and Paxton, all parties indebted to me, please call and settle at once." Kemper left Valley Falls with considerably more than when he had come, but his ambitions remained the same: to start a business of his own, though this time he would pick a town to fit the size of his dreams. William Kemper was twenty-seven years old, and he and his family were going to Kansas City.

Kansas City was a boom town just gone bust when Kemper and his young family moved there in 1893. Two years prior to the Kempers' arrival, another young Kansan, William Allen White, had gotten a job on one of Kansas City's several newspapers. By then the boom was over. "Mortgage companies in Kansas City were tottering," White wrote in his autobiography. "Several banks were unstable, and everyone knew it. The merchants were having a hard time making collections. It was rough going for young lawyers and young doctors. The fat pickings had vanished, and only the stark white faces of many a financial and mercantile structure, of many a small industry, were left for the young cubs."

William Kemper brought to Kansas City a wife and a young son, plenty of ambition, perseverance, and a mind predisposed to changing

Night Firing of Tobacco,
(1943) oil and tempera,
18x29 in.,
Thomas Hart Benton

Land settlers who rushed into the northern strip of Oklahoma carried with them the hardy Turkey Red winter wheat, which had been brought to the United States from the Crimean plains in Czarist Russia by the Mennonites. The vigorous strain of wheat grew abundantly on Oklahoma land that many had thought was suitable only for ranching and grazing.

careers. Kemper took as a business associate DeForrest Piazzek—son of a Polish miller in Valley Falls—and became a grain trader. The Kemper Grain Company was organized in 1893 and rented offices on the fourth floor of the Kansas City Board of Trade Building. It was an opportune time to become a Kansas City grain trader. Kansas City was emerging as the largest grain-trading center outside of Chicago. Moreover, Kansas City was a growing grain market because of the opening of Cherokee Indian land during the 1892–93 Oklahoma land rushes. Many who staked claims were Kansas wheat farmers, and almost all of the wheat harvested in Oklahoma was sold and traded through the Kansas City Board of Trade.

The 1894 city directory listed eighty grain-trading companies, each with its office in the Kansas City Board of Trade Building because it was important to have offices near the trading floor. A business summary in the directory talked about "croakers" in the grain business who had predicted the failure of many grain firms. Grain trading in 1894 set new records, owing in part to the addition of four million bushels of wheat from the new Oklahoma lands. By 1899, Kansas City received 20.3 million bushels of wheat, 8.6 million bushels of corn, and 2.4 million bushels of oats.

The Kansas City Board of Trade was established by the grain traders themselves to formulate and enforce rules concerning trading practices, payment terms, and market regulations. When ballots cast by the board of trade members were counted in 1900, the thirty-four-year-old William Kemper

William T. Kemper immediately became a grain trader when he moved to Kansas City in 1893 and was elected president of the Kansas City Board of Trade in 1900. The bustling trading floor, shown here as it appeared in 1910, was located at Eighth and Wyandotte streets.

had been elected its president. In six short years, Kemper had established a reputation for fairness and friendliness in the competitive grain-trading business. The presidency of the board of trade was a one-year term, but it was no small responsibility. The directors of the trade board met regularly to settle disputes between grain traders, railroad companies, and elevators. They also conducted informal trials in which the accused party was given an opportunity to plead guilty or not guilty to the charges.

Kemper, while devoting his primary attention to grain trade, did not abandon his other business interests. In 1895, the Valley Falls newspaper contained a notice from Kemper, who wanted it known that he had "money to loan at the lowest possible rates on improved farm property." Though he had started the company, William Kemper eventually turned control and operation of Kemper Grain Company over to business associates and shifted his business interests to mercantile trade. In 1900, Kemper and his uncle Thomas Paxton bought a department store located at Sixth Avenue and Quincy Street in Topeka from the Tanner brothers. The store's name was changed to Paxton and Paxton seven years later when Daniel Paxton, another relative of Kemper's mother, bought out Kemper's interest. In 1904, Kemper Mercantile Company was incorporated in the state of Missouri with a capital stock of $50,000, with each share having a par value of $100. William Kemper's father James owned 490 out of the total of 500 shares issued. The purpose of the company was to "carry on a general merchandise or mercantile business" of retailing and wholesaling while maintaining branch stores at various locations.

James Kemper moved to Kansas City in 1904 to be close to his son William and to become president of Kemper Mercantile Company. The business was in the 300 block of West Sixth Street, located in the West Bottoms

In 1900, Kansas City produced a fact sheet that boasted about how the city "ranks with the best" among United States cities in a number of categories. Kansas City had the second-largest livestock market, the second-largest rail center, the second-largest packing center in the world, and was the largest city west of Saint Louis.

near the train depot and the meat-packing plants. The next year, Kemper Mercantile moved to larger quarters at 1423–1441 West Ninth Street. Daniel P. Paxton, who had been partners in the Valley Falls dry-goods store with William Kemper, later replaced James Kemper as president.

Kemper Mercantile operated its own mail-order house and produced its own mail-order catalog that offered everything from pins to buggies. The Kansas City mercantile company tried the same marketing approach that had been pioneered by the Chicago-based concerns of Montgomery Ward and Sears Roebuck. By eliminating the middle man, the catalogs allowed farmers and other rural residents a wider selection of goods at prices that were lower than at the local dry-goods store. Unfortunately, all of the Kemper Mercantile Company catalogs have long since been destroyed, and the few remaining business records shed little information about why Kemper Mercantile was later sold to Lawrence M. and J. Logan Jones. Later, Kemper was to say, "When I left that early mail-order field, I stepped away from the chance to be a really rich man."

While lending his name and advice to the other businesses, Kemper had put his own money into the William T. Kemper Grain Elevator Company, which was incorporated in January of 1905 with a capital stock of $100,000. The par value of a share was $100. Kemper owned 497 shares, but the controlling interest belonged to Bruce Inman, who owned 500 shares. By April 1906, when the company voted to reduce its capital stock to $25,000, Kemper owned 997 of the 1,000 shares of stock. The grain elevator was located in the Missouri River bottoms along the Missouri Pacific Railroad tracks near Monroe Avenue. The name was changed to Kemper Mill and Elevator Company in 1908.

Kemper's main business interest was a company incorporated in 1902 that he named The Kemper Investment Company. Established with a capital stock of $50,000, Kemper owned 496 of the 500 shares, which had a par value of $100. The company's purpose, stated in the articles of incorporation, was to "buy, own, mortgage or sell real estate and other property . . . to negotiate loans and loan money on real estate; to deal in notes, bonds and other securities and commodities; to act as agent and broker and charge commission(s). . . ."

Kemper oversaw his many business enterprises from his main offices in a six-story brick building at 720 Delaware, appropriately named the Kemper Building. Helping to run the companies was a small handful of trusted associates including H. J. Diffenbaugh, DeForrest Piazzek, E. O. Bragg, Daniel Paxton, W. A. Hinchman, Benjamin Paxton (another brother of Kemper's mother), and W. O. Thomas.

The Paxtons were good retailers. One of the female relatives of Sallie Ann Paxton, Kemper's mother, married the father of another retailer who established an impressive mail-order and merchandising business that still bears his name—J. C. Penney. Because their mothers were related and they had grown up together around Hamilton, Missouri, William Kemper and J. C. Penney considered each other cousins. William Kemper was a success-

Rural Free Delivery, *(1936)*
oil, 12x26½ in.,
Kenneth Adams

ful Kansas City businessman when J. C. Penney in 1902 invested $500 in his first store, located in the Wyoming mining town of Kemmerer and named the Golden Rule Store.

William Kemper had begun to "strike out" into the world of politics, an unquenchable life-long passion. Kemper did not share the political views that his wife Lottie adopted from her father Rufus Crosby, who had been a rabid Republican. Kemper had been in charge of the big victory celebration in November 1892 in Valley Falls when the Democrats and Populists scored a stunning statewide victory. The Populists had swept to victory in most of

the statewide offices. Support for the Populist Party had been so strong in Kansas in 1892 that its presidential candidate, General James B. Weaver of Iowa, actually had carried the state.

Kemper showed the influence of Kansas populism when he emerged on the Kansas City political scene. In 1900, Kansas City hosted the Democratic National Convention. Kemper, as president of the Kansas City Board of Trade, arranged rental of cots to provide housing for grain dealers who wanted to see William Jennings Bryan secure the Democratic nomination for the second time. Because he was a prominent local Democrat and

County Politics, *(1952)*
lithograph, 13¾x16¾ in.,
Thomas Hart Benton

businessman, Kemper had his own booth to which he invited friends and business associates. One of those invited to the booth was an eastern Jackson County farmer and wheat trader named John Anderson Truman, whose sixteen-year-old son Harry served as a page circulating on the convention floor. "I'm afraid as a page I was a dud, but I ran many errands for Mr. Kemper," Harry Truman recalled long after having been elected to the very office that had eluded Bryan. Thousands crowded into the convention hall to hear Bryan, a brilliant orator, give his nomination speech after having been selected as his party's standard bearer by acclamation. "There were no loudspeakers, and a man had to have a real carrying voice to be heard in that hall. . . ." Truman recalled. "His appeal that day was like nothing else I have ever heard."

Kemper continued to be politically active and was appointed by the governor to the Kansas City Board of Police Commissioners. In 1904, only

eleven years after moving to Kansas City, Kemper won the Democratic nomination for mayor, though his selection resulted in a factional split. Not only was Kemper opposed by two important Democratic factions—those headed by Joe Shannon and by former mayor George M. Shelley—but he also had fierce editorial opposition from the *Kansas City Star*, which Kemper welcomed. "The *Star* as a political factor in our city, is death to whomsoever it smiles upon," Kemper said, "because of the fact that the taxpayers and people of our city have found through its record in past years it has not been their friend, but has ever fought the cause of taxpayers of the city in behalf of invidious interests."

His campaign platform called for more taxes to be paid by the public utility corporations, in particular the Metropolitan Street Railway Company, which controlled nearly all the streetcars in Kansas City. The Democratic split assured Kemper's April 1904 defeat to Republican Jay H. Neff, who polled 11,394 votes to Kemper's 9,929 total. Defeat left Kemper drained but undaunted. Two years later, he was back in the political arena again seeking the Democratic nomination for mayor. This time he was a much more forceful, outspoken candidate, particularly against those he felt had wronged him two years previously. Kemper's nomination was opposed by Democratic political bosses Joe Shannon, Jim Pendergast, and Fred Fleming, who had lined up behind another candidate, Robert L. Gregory.

Kemper left little to inference in his hard-hitting, rousing speeches befitting the style and traditions of the finest orators of Kansas Populists.

On April 4, 1900, the new Kansas City convention hall, which had been completed the previous year, burned to the ground just three months prior to the Democratic National Convention. The town responded to the disaster by hurriedly rebuilding a new convention hall on the same site using funds from the insurance company settlement and $150,000 raised through a community drive.

He said his candidacy represented "The People versus The Bosses," and he made it clear that the political bosses opposed his nomination because he had "no ambitions to wear the shackles of a political slave." Kemper appealed to honest people to reject Gregory as being no more than a pawn of the political bosses. If elected mayor, Kemper promised to appoint to office only qualified people who had "an honest personal and private record." Kemper said "bossism" had been "dethroned" in New York, Philadelphia, Baltimore, Boston, Cincinnati, and Saint Louis, adding that it was time to do away with bossism in Kansas City too.

Having been assailed by Kemper, the bosses fired back at the self-styled reformer. Various leaflets, circulated by Gregory's political friends, suggested that Kemper was the candidate of the hated Metropolitan Street Railway Company and criticized his performance as a police commissioner. Kemper lost the Democratic nomination; and Gregory, in turn, lost the general election to Henry Beardsley, a reform-minded Republican lawyer.

By this time, William and Lottie Kemper's family included three sons—Rufus, James, and William, Jr.—and a fine home in the 2600 block of Troost Avenue, where Lottie had begun collecting art and antiques. In business, the forty-year-old Kemper was well established in the grain trade and had expanded into merchandising with the mail-order house in the West Bottoms. But these business interests offered little challenge when compared to the opportunity that Dr. William S. Woods offered to Kemper

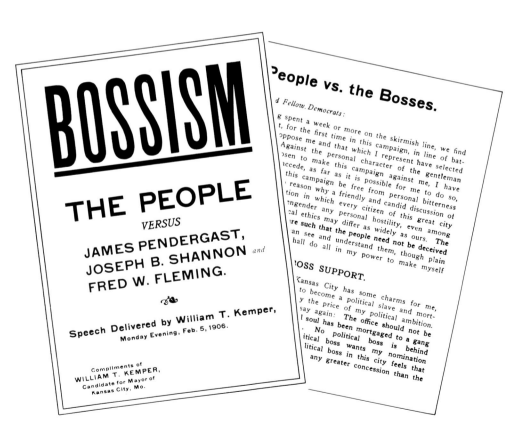

"I am opposed to having it understood that Kansas City is a boss-owned city. I am opposed to having its public servants boss-owned slaves."

William T. Kemper, *1906*
Kansas City mayoral campaign

Campaign brochure, 1906

*Seventeenth Street and Grand
Avenue, looking north in 1909*

*In 1909, L. K. Meek, a bank
employee in Oklahoma, sought
William Kemper's financial
advice. Kemper advised the
twenty-eight-year-old young
man to "go down in Oklahoma,
buy a little bank, and grow
with the country." Meek
considered the advice a cordial-
ity and began looking for
employment in Kansas City.
Feeling discouraged, he later
returned to Kemper, who asked
why Meek had not taken his
earlier advice. Meek responded,
"It's easy to say I should buy a
bank, but what could I use to
pay for one?" Kemper replied,
"Why, I intended to let you
have the money ... go to
Oklahoma, pick out a good
little bank, and if it's all right
I'll let you have the money to
pay for it." Meek followed the
advice and became a successful
Oklahoma banker.*

one day at the Kansas City Board of Trade. Dr. Woods, a strong-willed physician, was the dominant force behind the Bank of Commerce. He wanted a
bright, personable, and aggressive businessman to help form a related financial institution to be known as Commerce Trust Company. Woods went
looking for an alter ego; Kemper was his choice.

Woods, who had been a practicing physician, was a man people
"loved and feared." He had dominated the bank since 1882 when he had
gained control of the Kansas City Savings Association and changed its name
to the Bank of Commerce. Criticism by bank directors was not tolerated, but
Woods invested considerable authority in men that he trusted. Kemper
quickly secured both wide-ranging authority and unlimited trust.

When Commerce Trust Company opened for business in October
1906, Dr. Woods was its president and Kemper vice-president. Fifteen years
had elapsed since Kemper had been in the banking business with his father-
in-law Rufus Crosby, and there was little comparison between the Valley
Falls Bank of Deposit and the newly formed Commerce Trust Company. The
Kansas bank had been a private institution with total deposits of less than
$100,000, housed in a two-story building in a town of 1,200. The trust com-
pany, with capital of $1 million, was building one of the first steel-skeleton
skyscrapers in Kansas City, which had a population of 150,000-plus.

Commerce Trust Company was organized primarily to build a large
bank building at Tenth and Walnut streets at a cost of $1.8 million.
The building was to be rented to the National Bank of Commerce, which by
then had obtained a federal bank charter. The trust company, though performing some banking functions, originally was not viewed as a major competitor to the National Bank of Commerce. When the trust company opened
in 1906, it had four employees. Kemper quickly changed that. By 1908, de-

posits at Commerce Trust Company had reached $8 million; and it had become a major lender in the grain and milling trade—industries with which Kemper was quite familiar.

Something else quite remarkable also happened. Kemper shaped the bank and its practices to reflect his own personality traits. Customers were called by their first names. Rather than remaining sequestered in an office all day, Kemper went to the bank early in order to complete paperwork so that he could be on the floor greeting customers when the doors opened at ten o'clock. Kemper went out of his way to make bank customers believe they were important, whether they were depositing money or seeking a loan. George Kopp, who started his banking career at the Commerce banking institution, readily recalled the advice of his old supervisor, "I remember what my old boss W. T. Kemper said to me: 'Find out what a man's made of. A person's character means more than his financial statement.'" Kemper took time to talk with everyone and rarely turned down requests for a few minutes of his time. His business opinions were so well respected that many came merely to seek his advice and counsel. Lengthy scrapbooks kept by Kemper contained page after page of business axioms, quotes, and bromides that the banker had saved. Of the hundreds of items, Kemper had underscored one in red pencil to stress the significance that he associated with the words: **"The greater the man, the more safe and confident you may feel to approach him for counsel."**

*K*emper's roaring success at Commerce Trust Company was gaining notice, not only within the Kansas City financial community, but elsewhere. Though no formal policy statement exists regarding his business beliefs, a Kemper style of banking evolved at Commerce Trust Company. Its hallmarks were highly personalized service, community involvement, innovative marketing, and close hands-on personal management by the person in charge.

Dr. Woods, who dominated the National Bank of Commerce, temporarily lost control of the bank during the financial panic of 1907. By quietly buying stock he regained control the following year and temporarily assumed the office of president until J. W. Perry was appointed. Perry at National Bank of Commerce and Kemper at Commerce Trust Company presided over the two related banks that jointly made up one of the largest banking institutions west of Chicago. Woods increasingly withdrew from management of the banks owing to ill health.

Commerce Trust Company's growth was attributed to Kemper's ability to get new deposits, while successive mergers were the primary means of growth at the National Bank of Commerce. In 1912, a merger with the Southwest National Bank in Kansas City resulted in a marriage of institutional names, so that the merged banks became known as the Southwest National Bank of Commerce. Kemper and Perry continued to build the two banks into dominant financial institutions with correspondent banking relationships reaching throughout the entire Southwest. However, the presence of two banks with different boards and divided ownership,

One of Kemper's sons remembered him telling bank employees that there were ten things they should try to remember. The items, which Kemper had clipped out of a magazine and pasted into his scrapbook, were probably those of Chicago retailer Marshall Field and easily summarized Kemper's own values on personal and business affairs.

Ten Things to Remember

The value of time
The success of perseverance
The pleasure of working
The dignity of simplicity
The worth of character
The influence of example
The obligation of duty
The wisdom of economy
The virtue of patience
The improvement of talent

existing side-by-side in the same building, caused problems. In January 1917, following a year of internal maneuvering, the fifty-two-year-old Kemper agreed to retire as president of Commerce Trust Company and sell his stock. The move was part of a plan that put the two institutions under common ownership and a consolidated board of directors, though they remained separate institutions. The arrangement created the seventeenth largest bank in the country, and the bank's lending limit was increased from $500,000 to $750,000.

As part of his retirement agreement, Kemper received a $200,000 bonus, agreed to stay on at the bank in an advisory capacity for two years, and pledged not to become an officer in another bank for three years. He also sold 2,275 shares of Commerce Trust Company stock at $325 per share to a syndicate of shareholders in Southwest National Bank of Commerce. Counting his bonus and the stock sale, Kemper received nearly $1 million for retiring. "I am doing it for the best interests of Kansas City," Kemper said, "It will give an institution to this city that can develop the resources of the Southwest better than a smaller institution." At his retirement dinner held at the Hotel Muehlebach, Kemper came dressed in overalls, sporting whiskers, and wearing a red bandana. It was the city boy's way of letting people know that he intended to retire to his 600-acre farm near Reddell, Kansas, about twenty miles outside Kansas City. Republican Mayor G. H. Edwards praised the Democratic banker, "If there were more men like him it would be possible to have cleaner politics and better government."

Kemper's retirement was short-lived. By summer, Kemper was invited to become chairman of the board of both Southwest National Bank of Commerce and Commerce Trust Company. "When I sold the larger part of my interest in the Commerce Trust Company the first of the year, I did not expect soon to engage again in the banking business," Kemper said, "but when strong men on the boards of the two institutions invited me to come back I felt it my plain duty to comply with their request." Kemper's quick return to banking brought a tongue-in-cheek compliment from a writer in the *Kansas City Post*: "Last Saturday the men who made the contract with Mr. Kemper to stay out of Kansas City banking for three years decided $200,000 wasn't much as compared to the value of the man."

Kemper, acknowledging the contributions of his mentor, changed the name of Southwest National Bank of Commerce back to National Bank of Commerce of Kansas City. "Had it not been for Dr. Woods' interest and confidence in me, I don't think I would have ever been a member of the biggest banking institution in the city," Kemper said.

When Kemper had resigned from Commerce Trust Company, speculation had grown that it would clear the way for Kemper to seek political office. The politicians began talking about running Kemper for governor. Kemper, perhaps still bitter about his previous political campaigns, responded that he would run for governor "when I get paralyzed on all sides so that I will not know what I am doing." He was more interested in his community than in holding elective office. "Whenever I have taken a part in

Rufus Crosby Kemper, Sr.

political affairs in the past I have tried to stand for the things that made politics better and if an active interest in the welfare of the town and the state can be called 'politics' I am going in for that," he said. The self-deprecating Kemper downplayed his own political influence in Kansas City and with Missouri Governor Frederick Gardner. To the press, Kemper deserved the distinction of being "the assistant governor and vice mayor." When presidents came to town, Kemper was on the platform; when the powerful met, Kemper was invited; and when politics were involved, Kemper had a say.

Kemper left his mark in other more enduring ways through the parental influence he exercised over his three sons—Rufus Crosby, James, and William, Jr. The elder Kemper taught the boys the value of hard work, honesty, a man's word, and public service. Because of the prominence of their father, it was easier for the Kemper sons to entertain dreams greater than owning their own peanut stand. Although able to afford private education, the boys attended Kansas City public schools and the University of Missouri. All three were tall and handsome; some were more athletic than others. William Kemper had always been a great physical culturalist, getting up at five o'clock each morning to do a half hour of situps and drink generous amounts of water, followed by a walk of several miles toward the office before being picked up by a car.

Rufus Crosby Kemper, who disliked his first name and chose to go by R. Crosby or merely Crosby, loved football and made the University of Missouri football team as a junior. His father was an enthusiastic fan and sometimes attended the weekend football games at Columbia, Missouri. A particularly proud father watched Crosby play starting tackle during his senior year when the Tigers suffered only one loss. Crosby had the dubious distinction of scoring the only touchdown in the team's sole loss—a 24-to-7 defeat to Illinois—on a tackle-around play.

Upon graduating from the University of Missouri in 1914, Crosby spent a year at the Wharton School of Finance at the University of Pennsylvania studying corporation finance, banking, and related subjects. William Kemper also saw to it that his son Crosby did not lack an education in the school of hard knocks, which the banker had considered so invaluable to his own business career. A great disciplinarian, William Kemper expected his sons to work hard and save their money. During those times, sons did as their father told them, particularly when their father was William T. Kemper.

After Crosby had worked a couple of weeks at Commerce Trust Company, he was sent to work at Kemper Mill and Elevator at his father's personal direction. Crosby was to look after the family's interest in the grain business, while William Kemper kept track of things at Commerce Trust Company. The assignment came as a tough blow for Crosby, who really wanted to be a banker like his father. Soon a younger and taller Kemper was seen hurrying around the Kansas City Board of Trade Building, buying and selling wheat; just as his father had done twenty-five years earlier. William Kemper had trusted management of his grain company to his old Valley Falls friend DeForrest Piazzek until he resigned to accept a high-ranking job

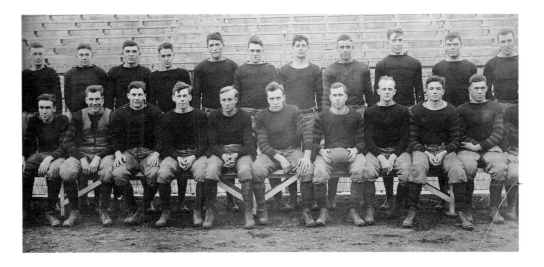

Informal team photograph of the 1913 Missouri Tigers football team. Crosby Kemper, Sr., who played tackle, is the third player from the right in the back row. In his senior year, Crosby, Sr. was selected to the third team of the All-Missouri Valley team.

at the United States Department of Agriculture. Piazzek had been recruited for the job because the United States was mobilizing troops, munitions, and foodstuffs to aid the war effort in Europe.

Despite strong isolationist sentiments within the country, the United States was being drawn inextricably into the armed European conflict that had begun with the firing of the guns in August 1914. In April 1917, President Woodrow Wilson went to Congress seeking a declaration of war so that the United States might fully enter into the conflict in hopes that doing so would "make the world safe for democracy." Young men everywhere responded to President Wilson's moralism and enlisted to fight in the "war to end all wars." Crosby and his brother James were two who answered their country's call; their younger brother William, Jr. was still a teenager. Though he enlisted as a private in the 140th Infantry, it was not long before Crosby was promoted to the rank of lieutenant—largely on the strength of military training in school—and was sent overseas to France. His brother James also served in France as a lieutenant in the balloon corps. For the United States, the war was short-lived. On the morning of November 11, 1918, generals met in a small railway car in the forest of Compiègne north of Paris and signed an armistice that ended the war. Early in 1919, Crosby and James returned to the United States within weeks of each other.

Following the armistice, Crosby assumed that he would return to the grain business. His plans were revised when a letter from his father arrived in France saying that Robert House, who had managed the grain company during the war, had died. It also appeared possible that the grain-export trade might be nationalized, and William Kemper wanted to get out of the grain business.

When Crosby arrived in Kansas City, his brother James had been installed as president of a small Kansas City bank controlled by their father William Kemper. The bank had the grand-sounding name of City Center Bank; but, compared to Commerce Trust Company and the National Bank of Commerce, the little bank easily was no bigger than a "peanut stand."

STARTING SMALL

William Kemper was a bargain hunter. Since his early days as a retailer, Kemper always had looked for bargains. As merchants, Kemper and the Paxtons had found failing stores, bought out their inventories at cents on the dollar, and then had pocketed the profits by moving the goods at sale prices. "My father was always buying stuff at receivers' sales," his son William Kemper, Jr. said.

The elder Kemper was no different when it came to banking. He had eyes for a small storefront bank at 1728 Grand Avenue. The City Center Bank was a rather nondescript, state-chartered institution not much bigger than the Valley Falls Bank of Deposit where Kemper had begun his banking career. Its total capital was exactly half of the $200,000 bonus Kemper received in 1917 to retire as president of Commerce Trust Company.

Kansas City was filled with small banks concentrated in the city's downtown financial district, but the poor little City Center Bank was an orphan child situated on the southern edges of the business district. The bank's most notable and distinguished neighbor was William Rockhill Nelson's newspaper, the *Kansas City Star*. A bank's name is often very descriptive of an institution's customers, primary purposes, geographic location, or self-aspirations; so when a handful of businessmen formed their own bank in April 1913, they named it the City Center Bank. Since 1853, when the "City of Kansas" was chartered by the Missouri legislature, the city had been growing progressively southward away from the Missouri River landings and the town's original settlement. Organizers of the new bank optimistically hoped that the southward expansion of the city's center would envelop their institution so that it eventually would be within the business and financial hub of Kansas City. Work was underway to complete Union Station, which was being moved out of the West Bottoms to a five-acre tract just southwest of the bank's location.

The bank was given its charter on April 24, 1913, by Missouri Bank Commissioner J. T. Mitchell, who charged $2.50 for the certificate and $75 for taxes, and assigned charter number 1921 to the bank. Starting a new bank was a popular, though not always profitable, business venture. City Center Bank's major stockholders were John A. Long, Fred S. Bullene, and

Portrait of Thomas Craven,
(1919) oil, 38x30 in.,
Thomas Hart Benton

Robert E. Booth. Each owned 286 or 287 shares of the 1,000 shares of stock issued by the bank. Long was president of Long Realty and Building Company and Long Brothers Grocery. Bullene evidently was a reporter for the *Kansas City Star*, and Booth had worked for the New England National Bank in Kansas City. The bank's board of directors was composed primarily of neighborhood businessmen: a grocer, a bottler, a car dealer, and an attorney. The board contained no prominent businessmen or representatives from major industries in the area.

In order to get its charter, the bank's three major stockholders—Long, Booth, and Bullene—filed a letter with the state banking commissioner showing that the City Center Bank had credit for $100,650 with Southwest National Bank of Commerce, the related institution to Commerce Trust Company headed by Kemper. At the end of its first year, City Center Bank reported total deposits of $277,072 with invested capital and reserves of $110,927, a small beginning for a bank supposedly at the city's center. For the first three or four years, the bank struggled to hold its own. In December 1916, the directors decided to raise the salary of the bank president from $1,200 annually to $1,800. "As the business of the bank is now on a steady earning basis, we feel this increase is only just to the officers and the employees," the directors reported.

In January 1917, Long resigned as bank president and was replaced by Booth. That fall Booth reported to the directors that the bank's net earnings were $7,246 for the first three quarters of that year. The bank had 1,181 checking accounts and another 559 savings accounts. The combined figures were up 312 accounts since the beginning of the year; and the following year, the directors approved an increase in the president's annual salary to $2,400.

Kansas City was emerging as a major banking center, particularly after its selection as a Federal Reserve Bank, which was rather a fluke. In 1913, when Congress approved a central banking system for the nation, the legislation established twelve separate Federal Reserve banks throughout the country. Saint Louis already had been assured of getting one of the Federal Reserve banks, so it was highly unlikely that Kansas City also would be chosen since it was in the same state just 250 miles to the west. Through extensive lobbying, Kansas City was selected along with the cities of Boston, New York, Philadelphia, Cleveland, Richmond, Atlanta, Chicago, Minneapolis, San Francisco, Dallas, and Saint Louis.

Kemper was an influential banker, widely known, politically well connected, and respected for his personal qualities; but he still did not have a strong ownership position from which he could protect himself and the institution he had worked so hard to build. Now Kansas City's influential banker saw a chance to have a bank of his own. Since City Center Bank's earnings had been weak during its first four years, Kemper was able to purchase the bank for cents on the dollar, have unquestioned ownership control, and provide career opportunities for his sons. City Center Bank fell into the hands of sharp-eyed bargain hunter William Kemper when he purchased a controlling interest in April 1918.

The original City Center Bank, located at 1728 Grand Avenue, was opposite the Kansas City Star Building. The bank also contained office space for Interstate Securities, an early car-financing company. William T. Kemper gained a controlling interest in this bank in the spring of 1918.

Kemper attended the April 16, 1918, board of directors meeting of City Center Bank along with Walter McLucas, his right-hand man at Commerce Trust Company. The minutes reported: "All the directors present listened, with interest, to the talk from Mr. W. T. Kemper as to the future policy of the bank and were assured by him that he and his associates wished to cooperate with the board of directors for the best interest of the institution and advised those present that his idea was for the directors to direct the institution and the officers to execute their direction." Young James Kemper was elected to the board of directors despite being out of town in the military service. James, a year younger than Crosby, had worked in a Kemper-controlled bank just prior to World War I.

The bank, prior to the ownership change, had resolved to move from its one-story location at 1728 Grand Avenue to a leased building half a block away at the southeast corner of Eighteenth and Grand. The board of directors, at its annual meeting in January 1919, also voted to change the bank's name to City Bank of Kansas City, thus ending the pretense that it was at the center of the city.

Though Kemper controlled the bank, he was in no position to manage its day-to-day affairs. He was receiver for a failed railroad, chairman of the boards of Commerce Trust Company and the National Bank of Commerce, and quite active politically. Kemper owned 280 shares of the bank, and his son James owned another 10 shares. The other major stockholders in

James M. Kemper, Sr.

1919 were developer J. C. Nichols (25 shares), Walter McLucas (50 shares), and John Groves (50 shares). The elder Kemper decided that James, who was a lieutenant in France, should head City Bank when Robert E. Booth, who had established the bank in 1913, retired as president in January 1919. The salary for the job was set at $2,500. Judge William Oliver Thomas was elected to run the bank until James Kemper returned from military service. The sixty-one-year-old Thomas had been an original director in The Kemper Investment Company and was a close personal friend of William Kemper.

*E*ven the best-laid plans of fathers go awry. James Kemper had been home no more than a month when he announced at a family dinner that he was resigning from City Bank and taking his wife, the former Gladys Woods Grissom, to Los Angeles. James Kemper's handwritten letter, dated March 6, 1919, informed the bank's directors of his plans:

Gentlemen:

Owing to the ill health of my wife it will be necessary for me to resign as President of the City Bank effective at once and move to California for permanent residence. I appreciate the honor conferred on me and in severing my connections wish the Bank the greatest success and prosperity.

James M. Kemper
President, City Bank

For Crosby, his brother's move to the coast meant the world. After his brother's resignation, Crosby took James's place at the bank after having first been elected to the board of directors and then given the position of president on March 11. Just weeks back from the service, the twenty-seven-year-old Crosby was president of a bank, however small. Crosby Kemper thus became the third generation of bank presidents in the family.

A Kemper-run and controlled bank was able to recruit more influential and affluent men to serve on its board of directors. Among those on the new board were George Hodges, a former Kansas governor; H. C. Blackwell, general manager of Kansas City Power and Light Company; R. P. Brewer, vice-president of National Bank of Commerce; and long-time Kemper business associate DeForrest Piazzek. The board retained some local businessmen, but the character of the bank and its board was changed.

The bank grew dramatically during 1919, partly owing to the war's conclusion. The Kansas City economy was strong as it reaped the benefits from the golden age of agriculture and being an early center for the new automobile industry. In March 1919, City Bank deposits totaled $574,319 and by November had doubled to $1,175,405. The November statement showed the bank had a capital stock of $100,000 and surplus and undivided profits of $29,072. By February 1920, deposits had inched up to $1,217,797, but the bank was able to increase its surplus and undivided profits to $38,130. That year the bank expanded next door into another storefront at 1807 Grand Avenue.

The Kempers' banking style and the outgoing personality of Crosby, who had gone into the endeavor with great energy and passion, also pro-

In 1919, the City Center Bank was relocated into larger, leased space on the southeast corner of Eighteenth Street and Grand Avenue; and the name was changed to City Bank.

vided impetus for the bank's rapid growth. At the time, Crosby lived at home with his family; and his younger brother William, Jr. remembers the vigor of the young banker: "[Crosby] had more books around the house on banking than you'd ever seen, and he was an inveterate reader of banking journals and all that stuff. He was great on getting out in the lobby, which his father did at Commerce Trust Company. My brother wouldn't have a private office, and my father wouldn't. My father was out there with the poor man and the rich man in the lobby. Crosby went down to Eighteenth and Grand and was greeting everybody; he was an extrovert."

Crosby turned for help at his new bank to the men that his father had trusted and taught the Kemper approach to banking. One of the bank's earliest employees was George S. Kopp, who joined the bank's staff as cashier in October 1920, replacing Roy A. Smith. Kopp was a man made

from the same mold as William Kemper: he had only a seventh-grade education, but was a good judge of character, loyal, and hardworking. "We saw to it that the small businessman had status in the bank," Kopp said about those early days at City Bank. "If he was ambitious and wanted to grow on a sound basis, he got credit. We wanted to grow with him."

Crosby had a great self-interest in the growing bank. Shortly after becoming president, he had gone to William Huttig, a friend at National Reserve Bank, for a favor. Crosby wanted to borrow $25,000 to buy City Bank stock, and Huttig obliged in grand style. Arriving at City Bank in a chauffeur-driven Pierce-Arrow, Huttig and his sons took Crosby Kemper to the infamous Chesterfield Club, a notable Kansas City hot spot, where the men celebrated Crosby's new career.

There were other reasons for Crosby to celebrate: the most important was his 1921 wedding to Enid Jackson of Tacoma, Washington. Crosby Kemper's engagement announcement was considered such prominent news that the Associated Press story ran on the front page of the *Kansas City Star*. A Kansas City society newspaper commented that "The future Mrs. Kemper is an Ogontz alumnus and one of those clinging-vine girls who generally capture an Apollo like Rufus Crosby." The banker gained a father-in-law who also was active in the grain business and a more ardent physical culturalist than Crosby's own father. Dr. Robert Jackson, Enid's father, was a physician and food faddist of missionary zeal. Fascinated with nutrition and diet, he spent hours in the family basement developing a breakfast mush that he called Roman meal because it consisted of whole-grain wheat, rye, bran, and flaxseed similar to what had been served to the Roman legions. He ate the mush regularly and started prescribing it to his patients. Jackson had set up a small factory in Tacoma to process Dr. Jackson's Roman Meal to meet the growing commercial demand. Dr. Jackson also produced a nutritious whole-grain bread; and in 1927 he sold the company to William Matthei, who had been a Kansas City baker.

The Kemper-Jackson wedding was held in Tacoma; and when the family returned to Kansas City, William Kemper offered his oldest son a house for a wedding present. Crosby had reservations about accepting the offer as he had toyed with the idea of asking his father instead for $10,000, the cash equivalent of the house, to invest in an interest-bearing account. Crosby, perhaps at the encouragement of his wife, decided that owning a home was preferable to renting.

Automobiles were changing American society, and Crosby understood that better than most. Not only did Crosby personally enjoy automobiles, but his City Bank was located along Motor Row, an area roughly bounded by McGee Street, Grand Avenue, and Sixteenth and Twenty-seventh streets. Crosby quickly made a name for himself with the car dealers. An automotive trade publication, *Motortrade*, in 1922 commented: "It may seem strange for a motor-trade publication to speak other than regretfully of a banker." The article praised Crosby Kemper's bank for keeping car dealers "off the rocks" during the previous two years.

In 1920, the rapidly growing City Bank expanded next door into the storefront at 1807 Grand Avenue. Bank president R. Crosby Kemper, Sr. and his employees are pictured in the window.

The state banking examiner, in his 1920 annual audit, criticized City Bank's large number of automobile loans: "A noticeable feature is a very large amount of automobile paper, $165,000.00 of which is secured by chattel mortgages on cars. Aside from being noticeable in amount I must with some degree look unfavorably upon the class of collateral that decreases rapidly in value." Roy A. Smith, the bank's cashier, responded: "We are located in the heart of the automobile district and are largely dependent upon these dealers for car deposits; of course, we must, in turn, take care of them by granting them loans if, in our opinion, they are financially responsible and [have] good and sufficient collateral."

Crosby Kemper purchased a car-financing company called Interstate Securities and provided offices for it at the back of the bank building. He then hired J. Frank Hudson, who had been an assistant credit manager at Commerce Trust Company, to run it. The typical financing plan, taken from a circa 1919 Interstate Securities brochure, required a 25-percent down payment and twelve monthly payments at 6-percent interest. From its inauspicious beginnings, Interstate Securities became an important means by which City Bank grew into a major financial institution. City Bank also helped newcomers get into the growing car business. Israel Bordman, a cigar merchant near City Bank, recalled: "I had a chance to make some car loans, and I went down to ask George Kopp what he thought of the idea. He encouraged me—helped me out in the first deals I made. . . ."

City Bank had strong ties with the Ford Motor Company through its close association with Interstate Securities. A full-page 1927 bank advertisement in the *Kansas City Star* stated that the 42,000 Jackson County residents who had not bought Ford cars had collectively wasted $42 million because, on the average, Ford cars cost $1,000 to $1,500 less than other car models. The ad reproduced a signed letter from Kemper stating that if the $42 million wasted by not buying less expensive but more reliable Fords had been invested in a regular savings account at 3-percent interest, it would have yielded $2,520,000 in interest income. "These figures are startling yet prove what money can do if wisely invested," the bank president importuned.

The 1920s were good times for Kansas City, which was well situated economically. It had a strong agricultural base, a transportation center, and a growing manufacturing sector partly related to the development of the automobile industry. The banks, in general, also prospered. The number of banks in Missouri peaked in 1920 when there were 1,535 state-chartered banks with deposits of $655 million and another 136 national banks with deposits of $324 million. City Bank with $100,000 in capital and $38,000 in surplus was an extremely small bank. The bank's most important intangible asset was the presence of the Kempers: the father as majority stockholder, son Crosby as president, and their distinctive banking style reflected in its operations. Crosby was the same kind of talented, aggressive banker as his father, but he was younger and taller.

William and Crosby Kemper were in financial control of City Bank. The elder Kemper held 40 percent of the stock while his son, using the money he had borrowed, had acquired 20 percent. A 1928 tax assessment, listing the stockholders of Kansas City banks, shows that William Kemper owned 900 shares of City Bank and his son owned another 462 shares. William Kemper and his son Crosby would build City Bank. Its success would be a credit to their names; its failure, a blow to their pocketbooks.

Commerce Trust Company, indeed, had been a remarkable success; but William Kemper had had the support of the National Bank of Commerce and Dr. Woods, a prime location in the downtown financial district, and an initial capital of $1 million. Crosby had the support of his father, a less advantageous location, and only $100,000 in capital. In 1921, the National Bank of Commerce and Commerce Trust Company merged under the latter name. The merged Commerce bank and First National Bank of Kansas City dominated banking in Kansas City and were considerable financial forces throughout the Southwest.

The merger created problems and internal policy dissents. Interests led by Theodore Gary, who had amassed a tremendous fortune through ownership of telephone systems, gained control of the bank by purchasing the stock held by Kemper, the chairman of the board, and J. W. Perry, the bank president. Approximately 10,000 shares of stock valued at more than $2.25 million were involved in the 1922 ownership change. No longer chairman of Commerce Trust Company, William Kemper was free to use his banking experience, contacts, and financial acumen to help build City Bank.

A portrait of the Kemper bankers, from left to right: William T. Kemper, Jr.; William T. Kemper, Sr.; R. Crosby Kemper, Sr.; and James M. Kemper.

In June of 1922, the City Bank board of directors agreed to build a new bank building sometime before 1934.

At Commerce Trust Company, bank officers were getting a little concerned about William and Crosby Kemper's growing little bank at Eighteenth and Grand. In December 1925, the Commerce Trust board of directors took the unusual step of making thirty-two-year-old James Kemper president of the bank. His selection as president made James one of the youngest managing officers of a major bank anywhere in the United States. James—who had worked for Commerce Trust since returning from California—was as capable a banker as his older brother, though less outgoing than either his father or Crosby. The suggestion that young James Kemper might one day head Commerce Trust Company would have surprised no one; but his selection at age thirty-two implied an effort to neutralize his father, should William Kemper ever entertain any ideas of throwing all his influence, contacts, and money into seeing City Bank become a head-to-head competitor with Commerce Trust Company.

James Kemper's selection as president of Commerce Trust Company hurt Crosby's feelings, fueling a deep-seated competitive drive to insure that someday his little City Bank would be the equal of Commerce Trust Company. In 1925, the idea truly was a wild-eyed dream. "[My father] was the oldest son, and he had the little bank, and his kid brother took over the big bank," according to R. Crosby Kemper, Jr. "Most people thought Dad was the younger son for that reason." William Kemper loved and admired his sons, but felt something special toward Crosby. "There's a big boy," said William Kemper as he directed a reporter to a picture of Crosby hanging on the wall. "That boy is a banker from his head to his heels, and that's a long way. I consider his banking success the greatest any man ever has achieved

in Kansas City. Besides making such a success, the big kid is really serving an important section of the city, the big fellows and the little fellows alike."

The elder Kemper, known by many as "Banker Bill," also shared his ideas about banking with the reporter. "It makes me sick to hear bankers boast of their small losses," he said. "I wouldn't give fifty cents for a bank's future or its value to the city if it didn't accept character as collateral and give every worthy chance a tryout." City Bank was growing with the support of small businesses and car dealers. Kansas City's big businesses might borrow their money or deposit their receipts elsewhere, but City Bank was willing to help prepare their payrolls, which in those days were payable in cash.

When the bank closed its doors in the afternoon, the proverbial banker's hours were just beginning for Crosby Kemper and George Kopp. They and other bank officers went door-to-door seeking new business and finding out what services customers were looking for from a bank. City Bank conducted new business campaigns, the spirit of which is reflected in a December 1928 bank report on a campaign: "In the bank here, new leaves are put in every ledger the first of the year. Add a new leaf to your daily ledger of life. Go after those new accounts, add some new names on these new leaves. If you haven't had the necessary enthusiasm, acquire it by practice, by application, by endeavor to succeed in this great sport of **Business**. 'Smoke out' the hidden funds that should be in your bank."

*C*rosby Kemper—like his grandfather—believed in "strict and true banking rules and regulations" but was willing to offer innovative banking services if they were not in conflict with those principles. The best example is City Bank's early involvement in drive-in banking. No one remembers where the idea originated, but in January 1931 City Bank cut an opening in the back door for an outside cashier's window so that customers could handle banking transactions without having to park their cars and go inside. The window might have been used no more than four or five times a day, but City Bank touted the window as an example of its willingness to serve its customers. A trade publication heralded the new service by picturing it on the front cover. "This is an age of superior service and accommodation!" *Bank News* reported. It was the first drive-in bank in Kansas City and believed to be one of the first in the nation.

City Bank enjoyed steady growth and strong profits, and its directors decided to undertake the new building they had first discussed in 1922. The Kansas City architectural firm of Holden, Ferris and Barnes was retained in 1926 to design a new bank building for the same corner as the existing building. The final design was for a seven-story building, though the steel skeleton ultimately could support thirteen stories. Architecturally, the building strongly reflected the pervasive influence at that time of the Chicago School of Architecture and its leading proponent, Louis Sullivan. The building was later judged by the Business District League to be the second-best downtown building constructed during 1927–28.

The basic design was a U-shaped building set upon a two-story main floor constructed of red granite. The upper floors were designed as

In 1931, City Bank's drive-in window was thought to be one of the first in the nation. Customers drove up to the window in back of the bank building and rang a bell that summoned a bank teller to handle transactions through the window.

rental office space. The bank's interior was luxuriant, with extensive use made of marble, walnut, brass, and wrought iron; and the exterior was intended to complement the brick facade of the Kansas City Star Building across the street. The lobby contained a beamed ceiling from which hung large, ornate-brass Art-Deco lighting fixtures. Most banking business took place on the 9,700-square-foot main floor, but in the basement was a huge steelcrete bank vault manufactured by Wheeling Corrugating Company.

When construction began on the new building in the spring of 1926, City Bank temporarily relocated to a four-story building on the northeast corner of Eighteenth and McGee streets, which provided the bank with more space than in its old building. During the sixteen months in the temporary quarters, the bank staff was not idle. Deposits increased by $1 million, and the number of employees increased from forty to fifty.

The doors of the new bank opened on July 18, 1927. The profusion of flowers and plants created an atmosphere more fitting for a grand funeral than the grand opening of a new bank building. Guests were given red carnations, and the men received special cigars for the occasion. An orchestra played music in the bank lobby that afternoon and later in the evening. The opening was such a significant community event that a dinner program featuring speeches by officers and directors was broadcast over radio station WHB. Roughly 15,000 people visited the bank before its doors closed at 10 P.M. that opening day. Crosby Kemper had arrived as a major city banker.

City Bank finally had an impressive building to demonstrate that it was one of the bigger, if not better, banks in Kansas City. In 1927, the stockholders voted to increase the capital stock from $100,000 to $300,000. The vote was 853 shares in favor to none against. At the year's end, the bank had deposits of $7 million. There still was no question that First National Bank and Commerce Trust Company dominated Kansas City banking, but City Bank was steadily building a base for itself.

Between 1926 and 1928, the bank stimulated growth by expanding its services to include a correspondent banking department, a farm loan department, a trust department, and a bond department. The trust department was established on the mezzanine level of the new building in 1927, after receiving approval from the Missouri Department of Finance to "exercise all the fiduciary powers now exercised by trust companies." Judge Thomas, who had run City Center Bank while James and Crosby were in military service overseas, headed the trust department. "All consultations confidential and without charge," the bank advertised. The bond department was opened on March 15, 1928, to specialize in high-grade government, municipal, corporate, railroad, and real-estate bonds. Hired to head the department was the affable and nattily attired bachelor F. D. (Donovan) Farrell. In announcing the new department, the bank said: "We shall try and safeguard our offerings with the most careful scrutiny and investigation that has characterized our securities for the past fifteen years."

It was a familiar story: being small meant working harder to get ahead. A bank officer from a later period recalled that over the years the ap-

POST "HOME EDITION

GANG RAIDS CITY BANK, SEIZING $20,000 IN LOOT AFTER FIRING ON WORKERS

"Seven men, according to several witnesses, raced into the bank with revolvers, automatics, pump-guns and a machine gun. Three bandits stood outside and two others were at the wheels of the waiting Buick sedan and a Packard. It was a swirl of looting, scuttling, shooting under the brilliantly lighted chandeliers and interior of the City Bank's proud lobby."

Kansas City Star,
February 24, 1928

During the grand opening on July 18, 1927, the lobby of the new seven-story City Bank Building at Eighteenth Street and Grand Avenue was decked with a profusion of flowers sent by well-wishers. Guests were greeted with red carnations for their coat lapels, and men were offered cigars.

proach to developing growth had remained the same: "We'd go hustle, hit the streets, and bring in customers the next day and have them in for lunch. We really built the bank that way, by personal contact." Bank employees recall Crosby Kemper saying, "The bank's open as long as somebody's in the bank or there is an officer to take a deposit to help you." Customers, on occasion, knocked on the bank door after the daily closing at 2 P.M. and were admitted to complete their business.

The day of February 24, 1928, was an entirely different matter. That morning two cars carrying twelve men pulled up in front of City Bank. Seven men dashed into the lobby, pulled guns, and robbed the bank of $50,737. Details of the "flashing robbery," including diagrams of the bank lobby, were the main story in the afternoon newspapers. The robbers, "shouting like cowboys," fired several warning shots; but no one was hit. Bank employees, including Crosby Kemper, were forced to lie down on the bank floor. Though the loss was covered by the bank's insurance, the whole

episode was quite unnerving. Kansas City police commissioner M. A. O'Donnell recommended that a bank's "best protection" against future robberies was construction of an armored cage staffed by a full-time security officer. Just four days after the robbery, City Bank's architects had completed sketches for a reinforced-steel guardhouse with gun slots cut in the sides that was quickly constructed on the mezzanine.

The year 1928 marked a profitable conclusion to a business venture for which William Kemper had risked his personal fortune, damaged his health, and invested a decade of tireless effort. Saving the ill-fated Kansas City, Mexico and Orient Railway had required Kemper to be an international diplomat, a financier, a promoter, a liquidator, a receiver, a litigant, a political lobbyist, an extraordinary negotiator, and president of a railroad. In late October 1928, Kemper sold his majority interest in the Orient to the Atchi-

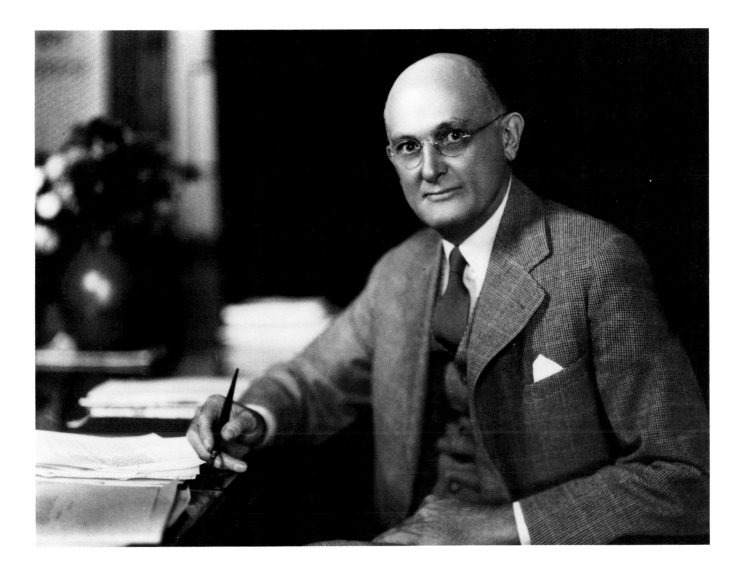

William T. Kemper, Sr.

Between 1906 and 1912 about eight miles of roadbed were graded to lay track in Kansas City, Kansas, in anticipation of extending the eastern terminus of the Kansas City, Mexico & Orient Railway from Wichita to Kansas City. About $1.8 million was spent on the unfinished Kansas City segment—known as the Kansas City, Outer Belt and Electric Railroad—before it was sold in 1922 for $350,000 by William Kemper, the railroad's receiver.

son, Topeka and Santa Fe Railway for $8.6 million—a considerable return for the $1.6 million that had been invested to buy up discounted notes of the Orient railroad during its darkest days. The sale immediately made Kemper one of Kansas City's richest men, adding considerably to the wealth he had already made in banking.

The Santa Fe railroad paid out another $6 million to English bond-holders, many of whom had been captivated originally by the dream of Kansas City railroad entrepreneur Arthur Stilwell to build a 1,610-mile railway from Kansas City across the Sierra Madre to Topolobampo Bay, a deep seaport on the Gulf of California in Mexico. Stilwell had promoted the railroad as the shortest distance to the Pacific.

More than 950 miles of rail line had been constructed over a ten-year period by the time the railroad went into receivership in 1912. Kemper served on the reorganization committee when the railway was reorganized in 1914–15 and another $5.6 million in bonds were sold, mostly in Europe. The railroad was unable to pay off the two-year notes in 1917, and again the Orient went into receivership. Kemper had just resigned his position as

Running Horses, *(1955)*
lithograph, 12½x16½ in.,
Thomas Hart Benton

president of Southwest National Bank of Commerce and agreed to become receiver of the railroad on April 16, 1917. For the next decade Kemper struggled to keep alive the railroad described by detractors as "two streaks of rust" that "started nowhere and ended at the same place."

On four different occasions, serious consideration was given to selling the rail lines for scrap. Between 1915 and 1922, the railroad racked up operating deficits totaling more than $3.7 million. Rather than purchase new equipment for the Orient, scrapped engines and cars were overhauled at Wichita machine shops; depots and shops were constructed out of demolished freight cars; cattle guards were made from demolished locomotive boiler plates; and short rails were sawed into posts. Railroad employees, like those at Kemper-operated banks, were encouraged to become strong salesmen for their employer. "Every employee has within his power the influence necessary to obtain additional business," Kemper wrote to the Orient employees in October of 1925.

The discovery of oil, more than efficiency, actually saved the railroad. Drillers in West Texas struck oil; and effective with 1924, the railroad began showing an increase in gross revenue. Because the railroad had not repaid a $2.5-million equipment loan granted by the Interstate Commerce Commission, the government foreclosed on the railroad in February 1924 and offered it for sale. The railroad's general counsel Clifford Histed, acting as Kemper's agent, bid $3 million. A year later when the bid was approved by a federal judge in Kansas City, Kansas, Kemper reorganized the railroad and installed himself as president. His sons James and Crosby were on the board; and William, Jr. worked as an assistant to his father. Though the railroad was something of a family affair, it provided little fun and even less profit. The best hope was to sell the Orient to another railway, but initial approaches to Missouri Pacific were rejected before a deal with the Santa Fe was completed. At the negotiated sale price of $414.40 per share, Kemper profited quite handsomely from the purchase of his 20,439 shares. He had turned somebody else's considerable failure into his own roaring success with the help of some good timing.

It was a fortuitous time for Kemper to sell the railroad. Twelve months later, wealthy men saw their paper fortunes crumble beginning with the collapse of the New York Stock Exchange on October 29, 1929, a day thereafter known as Black Tuesday. Within two weeks, over $30 billion in the value of listed stocks was wiped out. The stock market crash set off reverberations throughout the entire country that shook the foundations of many financial institutions, including the Kemper banks.

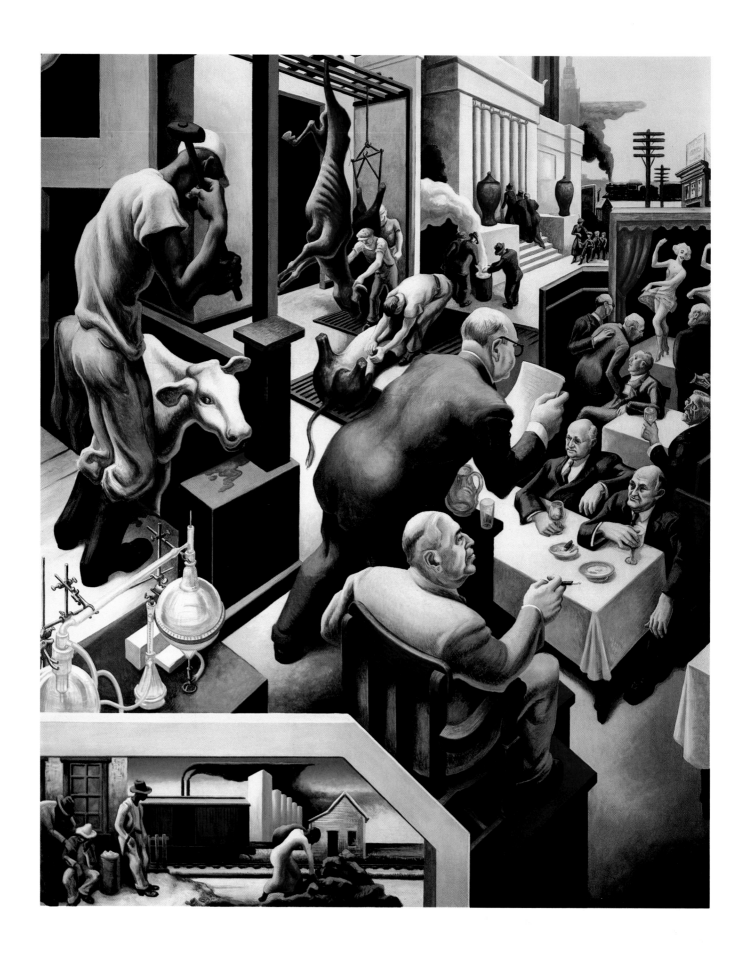

~4~

R. Crosby Kemper

BUILDING A FIRST-CLASS BANK

Throughout the city, bankers spent the Sunday evening of March 12 close to their telephones anxiously waiting for the word. By order first of Missouri Governor Guy Park and then of President Franklin Roosevelt, all of the bankers had closed their bank doors to business for a week as part of a government-declared bank holiday effective March 6, 1933.

That evening most of the bankers, along with millions of their fellow citizens, gathered in their living rooms to listen to the radio as the newly inaugurated Franklin Roosevelt gave his first fireside chat, a short public discourse on banking. "Because of undermined confidence on the part of the public, there was a general rush by a large portion of our population to turn bank deposits into currency or gold—a rush so great that the soundest banks could not get enough currency to meet the demand . . ." Roosevelt said, "I can assure you that it is safer to keep your money in a reopened bank than under the mattress. . . . Confidence and courage are the essentials of success in carrying out our plan. You people must have faith; you must not be stampeded by rumors or guesses. Let us unite in banishing fear."

City Bank, during the Herbert Hoover–depression years, had tried to protect its financial position by reducing its customer loans and increasing its investments. The bond market, however, was chaotic. One shareholder audit of City Bank during the period stated, "No attempt was made to place a value on the bond account. As you are aware, the bond market is depressed to the point that quoted values no longer represent actual values, a condition which is recognized by the Comptroller of the Currency and by our State Finance Department."

In 1931, bank profits for the $8-million City Bank and Trust Company totaled $8,081. The profits would have been substantially higher had it not been for a $144,380 loss in the bond department. During the first quarter of 1932, City Bank and Trust Company experienced a reduction in demand deposits of $945,000, about one-seventh of its total deposits. With fewer deposits, the bank reduced its loans and discounts by $738,000. Though City Bank and Trust Company was still profitable, measures were taken to operate the bank under "trimmed sails," as the board of directors placed a moratorium on salary increases and paid vacations. In July, the directors

economized still further by declaring that a 15-percent salary reduction for all employees "from president on down" was in order.

William Kemper, in a December 1931 article, had noted that the depression had been accompanied by disinflation and lower prices. "In a way, the depression is one of the best things that ever happened in the United States. It brought us to our senses. We were going too fast. It has been a severe lesson, but a valuable one," he said. Two years later, he was saying, "One of the things that is keeping back our progress is our lack of confidence. But we are overcoming this obstacle. Having reached the bottom, we know that any change must be for the better."

Hoover's presidency had been an unmitigated economic disaster since the collapse of the stock market in October 1929. The country and the economy steadily had moved into a devastating depression, and Hoover was unable to turn the economy around. Roosevelt hoped to halt the slide and instill a new confidence in the nation by comforting a distressed and depressed nation in his March 4, 1933, inaugural address. William Kemper was one of the thousands gathered that Saturday below the portico of the United States Capitol to listen as the newly sworn-in President Roosevelt told the nation: "Let me assert my firm belief that the only thing we have to fear is fear itself." One of the most pervasive fears was whether the banks would be able to pay depositors in full upon demand. The next day Roosevelt declared his bank holiday and called Congress into special session on March 9 to consider hurriedly drafted emergency banking legislation, which was debated and approved on that same day. The far-reaching legislation gave the president broad powers to control foreign currency exchange and gold exports, allowed the Comptroller of the Currency to take control of national banks, and permitted members of the Federal Reserve to use sound assets as collateral to borrow funds from the central bank.

Crosby Kemper, the forty-one-year-old president of Kansas City's fourth largest bank, listened to President Roosevelt that Sunday evening, March 12, on the radio at home with his wife and three children. He and other Kansas City bankers waited and wondered if the government would permit them to reopen their banks the next day following the conclusion of the government-declared holiday. The bankers had their answer around 9:30 P.M. via telegrams to the Federal Reserve Bank: the separate messages from Washington and Jefferson City contained the list of banks that were licensed to reopen the next day. The only banks not approved to reopen immediately in Kansas City, Missouri, were Fidelity National Bank and Trust Company, Missouri Savings Trust Company, and Fidelity Savings Trust.

The day before—Saturday, March 11—Crosby had called a special meeting of the board of directors for City Bank and Trust Company. After much discussion, the directors had agreed that the bank should join the Federal Reserve Bank System, which would cost $42,000 but would allow the bank to borrow money against its assets in order to meet demands of depositors and maintain its liquidity. It was the second serious matter resolved by the bank directors in a five-week period. On February 4, Crosby had con-

"Size makes delegated authority necessary. Naturally I want to see this bank continue to grow, but if it becomes too complicated for the personal relationships I will not enjoy my job as much as I do today."

Crosby Kemper, Sr., *1933*

The entire Kemper family gathered for an informal portrait in front of Charlotte and William T. Kemper's Kansas City home, about 1932. Back row, left to right: James "Big Jim"; Charlotte; William, Jr.; William, Sr. with Julianne and R. Crosby, Jr. in his arms; and R. Crosby, Sr. Front row, left to right: David (seated); James, Jr.; Gladys; Jan; Enid; and Sally Ann.

tacted several of the directors about an emergency situation at the Broadway Bank of Kansas City, located at the corner of Southwest Boulevard and Broadway Avenue. Founded in 1919, the Broadway Bank was about to go under but could be saved if a willing buyer could be found immediately. Acting quickly, Crosby had received approval by phone from his bank directors to buy Broadway Bank. "Economics and other factors that enter into consolidations made our merger into the City Bank advantageous," said Kearney Wornall, the president of the Broadway Bank who became a vice-president of City Bank and Trust in the merger. The catch-all phrase *other factors* glossed over the many financial difficulties facing banks everywhere—even strong, well-managed institutions like City Bank and Trust Company—in the aftermath of the 1929 stock-market crash.

Compared to the previous months, Monday, March 13, was a grand day for the twenty-four Kansas City, Missouri, banks that had received government permission to reopen. During the bank panic, many had gone to the financial institutions seeking to convert their currency into gold, which was the monetary standard at the time; but Roosevelt's fireside chat had partially allayed the nation's fears. On the day the banks reopened, a Kansas City newspaper reported: "Gold is coming out from hiding to add to the base for the country's currency. The trickle of gold back to the Kansas City Federal Reserve Bank is becoming a rich yellow stream."

Crosby Kemper stood in the City Bank lobby greeting customers who came laden with a week's worth of deposits that they had been unable to bank during the closure. The few withdrawals consisted largely of pocket money for depositors who had been unable to get cash during the week-long bank holiday. For many banks, the trickle of gold and currency back into their vaults was too late. Only strong banks could withstand the financial drain on their resources. However, by October 1933, Kemper was able to write to the Missouri banking commissioner, "If we were to liquidate this bank today, we could pay our depositors one hundred cents on the dollar and collect our entire Surplus and Capital Account of $700,000 and a large part of our Undivided Profits Account." Other banks were not so fortunate.

Crosby Kemper always sought for new ways to give his bank an institutional identity over and above the recognition it enjoyed because of the Kempers' banking reputation. The oldest Kemper son cast his eyes upon a bronze statue titled *The Scout* that had caught the fancy of Kansas City. The sculptor was a Utah native, Cyrus Dallin, who had been invited to exhibit his sculptures of American Indians at the 1915 Panama–Pacific Exposition at the San Francisco Fair. There Delbert J. Haff, a former member of the Kansas City Park Board, became enamored with Dallin's figure of a larger-than-life American Indian sitting bareback on a horse and peering toward the horizon. Returning to Kansas City, Haff launched a successful $15,000 public-subscription campaign to purchase the 3,500-pound statue and bring it to Kansas City, where *The Scout* was mounted on a granite pedestal in Penn Valley Park. Crosby Kemper was enthralled with the statue and toyed with the idea of using *The Scout* as a bank trademark. To him, *The Scout* was a symbol of the kind of bank he wanted to run. "An Indian scout was alert and, through experience and skill, was ahead of the rest of his people in knowledge of the country," Crosby once said.

Even the most sagacious scout would have had a hard time recognizing the economic landscape during the depression years. The banking industry was going through some fundamental changes as a result of major banking legislation enacted by the United States Congress. The new laws prohibited banks from paying interest on demand deposits and established a ceiling on interest rates for time and savings deposits. They also restricted the number of banks for which an individual could serve as an officer, employee, or director. That requirement prompted William Kemper, Jr., the youngest brother of Crosby, to resign from the board of City Bank and Trust

The Scout, *Cyrus Dallin*

The Scout *represented the sentiments contained in the turn-of-the-century "Epic of Kansas City," by poet C. L. Edson, whose rhythmic verses reflected the public perception of the western Missouri city at the time.*

> *Come Kansas City, make your story brief:*
> *Here stands a city built o' bread and beef.*
>
> *This is Kansas City, where the tribe trails meet,*
> *The rail head, the gateway, the West's Main Street,*
> *The old tribal stamping ground to stamp your feet.*

Company in January 1934 because of his involvement in other Kemper banks outside of the Kansas City area.

By the end of 1934, City Bank and Trust Company was a fundamentally different legal entity. The state-chartered bank had joined the Federal Reserve System, had made application to become a member of the Federal Deposit Insurance Corporation, and had decided to apply for a charter to become a national bank at a special meeting of the board of directors on the day after Christmas in 1933. On January 10, 1934, the United States Comptroller of the Currency notified the bank that its application had been approved and it had been granted national charter number 13,936. When the bank opened the next day, it added *National* to its name. Federal banking regulators informed the bank officers that in becoming a national bank, City Bank and Trust Company would have to increase its capital from $300,000 to $600,000. A motion to increase the capital was approved by the directors at their February 1934 meeting, but only after a lengthy discussion and dissenting votes cast by Don Ricksecker, the third largest stockholder in the bank behind William T. and Crosby Kemper.

During the depression many banks increased their capital by selling preferred stock to the government-backed Reconstruction Finance Corporation, a move that the government strongly encouraged as a way to undergird the banking system with the infusion of more capital. The Reconstruction Finance Corporation preferred for communities to reinvest in their banks by purchasing bank stock, which was the course taken by City National Bank and Trust. Crosby Kemper, in a newspaper statement, said: "The board of directors . . . preferred to give our present stockholders the privilege of subscribing to the new stock rather than sell preferred stock to the government through the Reconstruction Finance Corporation."

William Kemper had been rumored for various high-level appointments in the new Roosevelt administration, including the post of assistant secretary of war, head of the Reconstruction Finance Corporation, and other assignments. Kemper quickly responded to the rumors by saying, "I am staying in Kansas City and very contentedly staying. I would accept no position in Washington of any kind." Kemper had been a member of the Democratic National Committee since 1924; and the position gave him great influence in political appointments, candidate selection, and public issues, not only in Democratically controlled Kansas City and Jackson County, but throughout the state. The banker was quite close to James A. Farley, a Roosevelt confidant who had traveled the country as the New York governor's emissary prior to the 1932 Democratic convention in Chicago.

Kemper had worked quietly behind the scenes on behalf of Franklin Roosevelt's presidential candidacy, even though United States senator and former Kansas City mayor James A. Reed considered seeking the presidential nomination as a favorite-son candidate from Missouri. In August 1931, Kemper wrote to Roosevelt at the New York governor's mansion in Albany, "I have been in a quandary as to what should be done for you in the State of Missouri. The sentiment is favorable to you, and I would recommend that

William Kemper and Franklin Roosevelt had a little-known personal fallout after the 1932 Democratic National Convention, where Kemper had worked hard on behalf of Roosevelt's presidential candidacy. Following the convention in Chicago, Roosevelt summoned Kemper to the governor's mansion in Albany, New York. The banker sat on the veranda of the governor's mansion for his long-anticipated interview with Roosevelt. When the New York governor appeared on the veranda, he told his invited guest: "Mr. Kemper, I'll give you ten minutes to tell me about Missouri." The Kansas City banker took it as an affront and told his party's presidential nominee that he might want to find someone else to describe the intricacies of Missouri politics in the allotted time.

we start a movement in your behalf, if it were not for Jim Reed. . . ." Kemper said that as Democratic national committeeman his "hands were tied to a certain extent," but offered to have "younger men who will give a good account of themselves" start a Roosevelt movement in Missouri at any time.

Kemper remained quite close to Roosevelt's political confidants; and Jesse Jones, a Houston, Texas, lumberman and banker who headed the Reconstruction Finance Corporation, was indirectly responsible for Kemper becoming actively involved in banking again. In February 1933, the Reconstruction Finance Corporation and General Motors jointly created a new bank called the National Bank of Detroit that was to have an initial capital of $25 million. Jones asked William Kemper to suggest a midwestern banker to direct the new bank; and Kemper proposed Walter S. McLucas, president of Commerce Trust Company. McLucas accepted the formidable Detroit bank job and took with him two top banking officers from Commerce Trust Company. After McLucas left, the bank directors at Commerce Trust Company elected William Kemper to be chairman of the board. He assumed the post less than a month after the national bank holiday in March 1933.

The indefatigable Kemper returned to Commerce Trust Company with the same enthusiasm that he had infused into the organization years before. On the day the sixty-seven-year-old Kemper returned to the bank, a bank officer observed that "he's taking over that desk for the day. But he'll probably have two or three desks. It's pretty hard to keep him in one place. He likes to move around and to meet people." This time William Kemper was determined to consolidate the Kempers' hold on Commerce Trust Company. He was again chairman of the board, his middle son James was the bank president, and earlier that year his oldest son Crosby had been elected to be vice-chairman of the board. In reporting the appointment, the newspaper commented: "Placing Crosby Kemper in the vice-chairmanship was at once a gesture of courtesy to the City Bank head and a friendly recognition of the increased stock holdings of the Kemper family in Commerce." William Kemper actually had been buying back the Commerce Trust Company stock that he had sold to the Gary-led syndicate in 1922. In 1932, he reacquired for $86 per share the Commerce Trust Company stock that he had sold for $220 per share to the Gary interests ten years earlier.

*E*asily the largest shareholder of City National Bank and Trust, William Kemper retained an active interest in the bank's affairs. Long-time directors recall that the elder Kemper would never hesitate to question his son at meetings of the City National Bank board. Despite holding a seat at the directors' table at Commerce Trust Company, Crosby Kemper's heart always remained at the bank he had built—City National Bank and Trust Company. "I would rather be president of this bank than anything else in the world," said Crosby in 1933. "We have built this bank on personal contacts. We believe that many people would rather do business with human beings than committees. I know I would." In size, there was no comparison between the two Kemper-controlled Kansas City banks. The midyear 1934 financial statements for the two dominant Kansas City banks showed Commerce Trust

had total resources of $126.8 million, compared to First National's total of $107 million. City National Bank and Trust Company was the city's fourth largest bank with total resources of $16 million, but it was just one-seventh the size of Commerce Trust. So dominant were Commerce Trust and First National that the combined total resources of the other twenty-seven Kansas City banks added up to $117.7 million, or less than the total resources of Commerce Trust Company alone and only slightly more than those of First National Bank.

James Kemper, as president of Commerce Trust Company, was the city's highest-paid bank president in 1934, commanding a salary of $26,325. His father received no salary as chairman of the bank board, while his brother Crosby earned $12,750 in 1933 as president of City National Bank and Trust Company. The brothers were competitive, yet cooperative, and were even more so since their father William Kemper again had a large block of stock in Commerce Trust Company. Crosby Kemper loved to tell a story about how his brother James, known in the banking community as "Big Jim," had taken a bank account away from City National. A music store was located across Grand Avenue from Crosby's first-floor window in City National. Shortly after his brother had loaned the store money, it went broke and closed its door. Crosby, looking out his office window, saw his brother helping to carry musical instruments out of the store. He waited until he knew his brother had had time to get back to Commerce Trust and called: "Jim," he said, "which one of those instruments are you going to play? Are you going to play that tuba? I want to hear you."

Growth of City National Bank and Trust Company during the first decade of Crosby Kemper's leadership had been little short of phenomenal, but the depression had created conditions that made sustained long-term growth in net profits extremely difficult for banks. Crosby, the inveterate reader of banking journals and student of Wharton School of Finance, viewed the events philosophically. "I could not imagine more interesting times than this period from 1929 to 1933," he said. "Men who have survived have learned more than they learned in any other ten years of their business lives. I know I have. Without going through that period no man could have any conception of how fast things could slump or of how fast they could come back."

City Bank had grown during the 1920s by helping small businesses, making car and real-estate loans, and establishing bond and trust departments. During the depression, businesses had failed, car purchases had declined, the real-estate market had collapsed, and the bond markets had dropped to historic lows. Hard times did not idle Crosby's ambitions. Starting in the late 1920s, Crosby had begun to establish bank departments and assemble the men who would be instrumental in the bank's tremendous growth once economic fortunes improved. Kemper's associates remained largely intact through the mid-1950s and built the bank into an institution worthy of mention in the same breath as Commerce Trust Company and First National Bank of Kansas City.

"Grow with a Growing Bank. You'll like to do business with this bank. You'll like the spirit of achievement, the frank optimism, the will to get things done that pervades the entire organization. We're young, vigorous, growing—a bank with a future for men with a future."

City Bank advertisement, June 1927

Portuguese Mother and Child, *(1914) oil, 49x40 in., William M. Paxton*

James Samuel Neely, seated at the front desk, was the driving force behind the development of City Bank's correspondent banking department. Colleagues called Neely "Gentleman Jim"; and he was an avid baseball fan, having played semipro baseball as a youth. When Neely started in 1927, the correspondent banking department had $77,000 in deposits from eleven small-town banks. When he retired in 1960, City National Bank had deposits of nearly $68 million from more than 900 banks. Behind Neely in this 1927 photograph is cashier Ross Rheems. Against the back wall on the left is George Kopp; on right is R. Crosby Kemper, Sr.

F. Donovan Farrell, the son of an Oklahoma grocery salesman, made a name for himself in investment circles as a splendid dresser. Because he possessed a dynamic, though sometimes explosive personality, colleagues often joked that his first initials stood for "Fire Department."

Don Farrell, who headed the bond department, had an infectious personality and had gained a national reputation as a prominent figure in the Investment Bankers Association, an early industry trade group. Though the bank's bond department originally was quite small, Farrell was on a first-name basis with bond traders in the major banks throughout the country and believed that men, not machines, sold bonds. "The hell with the machines, buddy," Farrell told new bond salesmen. "All you need is that telephone. That's what you sell bonds with. Get on that telephone and get to work." The bank's early bond salesmen traveled widely throughout Missouri and Kansas to secure a large amount of bond business from small rural school districts and communities.

The bond department was a growing segment of the bank as lower incomes and the questionable credit-worthiness of customers curtailed wide-scale lending to individuals and businesses during the depression and World War II. Government bonds, on the other hand, were backed by the full faith and credit of a legal entity that could raise taxes to pay the interest and principal. During the depression and World War II, governmental debt held by the public increased in absolute terms and also as a percentage of the total credit market held by the public. That increase in percentage was reflected in greater activity by the bond departments, stockbrokers, and other securities traders throughout the financial industry.

he correspondent banking department had been organized in July 1927 by James S. Neely. He had come to City Bank after working nine years as an assistant cashier at Drovers National Bank. A first lieutenant in World War I, Neely had worked in Europe for several months following the war for the United States Food Administration. Neely was endlessly travel-ing to banking conventions and looking for more correspondent business. Kearney Wornall, who also worked in the department, was quite well edu-cated and bore the names of the two prominent pioneer Kansas City families from which he was descended. Trained as an attorney, Wornall had helped to start the Broadway Bank that merged with City Bank and Trust Company. Wornall traveled extensively in Missouri, Texas, and New Mexico in an effort to develop correspondent banking relationships.

The bank's greater interest in livestock loans, in turn, helped to ex-pand City National's correspondent relationships with small banks in the rural Southwest. A separate livestock loan department was formed in 1936 and was headed by J. Milton Freeland, whose family had run the Stock Yards Loan Company. The livestock loan company had been controlled by the major Kansas City meat packers but had failed during the depression. When the loan company closed, Crosby had hired Freeland and had the bank buy up some of the better loans. Even when the prime rate was only 1.5 percent, it was not uncommon for the interest rate on cattle loans to be 6 percent,

William T. Kemper, Jr.

because of the high risks involved in ranching. The interest spread made the livestock loans profitable, and Freeland's extensive knowledge of the ranchers throughout Missouri, Kansas, Colorado, Oklahoma, Texas, and New Mexico helped to assure that quality loans were made.

During the depression, the bank's real-estate department was reorganized as a separate legal entity called City Bond and Mortgage Company. The company continued to operate out of the bank building under the direction of William O. Norman, a long-time bank vice-president. The contract separating City Bond and Mortgage Company provided for a ten-year initial lease that required payment of 15 percent of the net profits to City National Bank and Trust Company. The bank's small trust department continued to be named executor in wills, but fee income from trust work was a long-term proposition for bank growth since the income was realized only after clients' estates were settled.

*D*espite the depression, City National Bank and Trust Company continued to show growth in its deposits. In the five years between 1928 and 1933, deposits had increased from $8.7 million to $10.0 million, or about 2.9 percent annually. However, in the next five years between 1933 and 1938, deposits more than doubled to $25.5 million, a five-year increase of $15.5 million or an annual increase of about 31 percent.

The men assembled by Crosby Kemper were aggressive, personable, and interested in their community. Crosby felt that involvement in a wide range of personal, professional, and community associations provided additional opportunities to promote the bank and cultivate new customers. Crosby Kemper once told a group of his banking officers who were attending a banking convention that not all of them were to sit at the same table. "Spread out boys," he said. "Lightning might strike." He fostered an underdog mentality that pervaded the organization for more than a generation. Because of its lower lending limit, City National was unable to provide the larger loans needed by bigger industries in Kansas City and the Midwest; but it was willing to provide any feasible service to establish a relationship so that in the future it might attract some of the business that was going to the downtown banks with higher lending limits.

Crosby Kemper played a key role in retaining control and headquarters of a major industry in Kansas City. The company was the Kansas City Southern Railroad, the railroad originally named the Kansas City, Pittsburg and Gulf. Unlike the Orient, the Kansas City Southern was a profitable railroad and provided rail services for a six-state area. Though most of its operations were centered in Kansas City, the corporate headquarters were in New York City where the business affairs were run by "an unchallenged czar" in the person of aging railroad man, L. F. Loree. Crosby Kemper was nominated to be a director of the Kansas City Southern by minority interests made up principally of partners in the stock brokerage firm of Paine, Webber and Company, which controlled about one-fifth of the railroad stock. With Kemper's election, the fifteen-member board of Kansas City Southern included four Kansas City businessmen. By 1936, the minority interests

Three generations of Kemper men, from left to right: R. Crosby, Jr.; James, Jr.; David; William, Jr.; James, Sr.; R. Crosby, Sr.; and William, Sr.

wanted to wrest control from the seventy-seven-year-old Loree, who personally owned five shares of stock but controlled thousands of proxies for Dutch stockholders. Crosby Kemper was viewed as the natural leader of the maverick minority interests. Loree emerged from the 1936 annual meeting with his job and $45,000 annual salary intact but by the end of 1936 had resigned and was succeeded by someone put forth by the minority owners.

The ever-vital William Kemper was beginning to tire. In 1936, he decided to retire as Democratic national committeeman after serving twelve years. His sons were a continual source of pride; and as he had also become a grandfather, William Kemper liked to take time to teach and tell stories to his grandchildren. On Sunday afternoons at the family home in the 1000 block of Westover Road, the venerable businessman would hold forth on banking, politics, and his early days of getting started in Saint Joseph and Valley Falls, Kansas. When politicians visited Kansas City—Farley, Jones, or Roosevelt's sons—they usually stayed at William Kemper's home. It was quite an experience for the grandchildren as their grandparents' house was an always-in-session school of practical learning. The grandchildren developed strong feelings of family loyalty; and important family values, such as personal integrity and hard work, were reinforced.

Building a First-Class Bank (1929-1938)

As City Bank continued to grow, a new seven-story bank headquarters was constructed on the southeast corner of Eighteenth Street and Grand Avenue. It opened in July of 1927 and was linked to the downtown financial district by a trolley-car system that ran north and south along Grand.

Rufus Crosby Kemper, Jr., the youngest child of Enid Jackson and Crosby, Sr., remembers visiting his grandparents at a vacation home in Southern California. "They hadn't made provisions for me and [my grandfather] found me washing my own clothes down in the basement. He never forgot that. He thought it was so industrious. He had a very strong work ethic, which I think has come down all through the family." Crosby, Sr. impressed the same qualities on his young son by working hard as president of City National Bank and Trust Company.

Increasingly, William Kemper left banking affairs to his three sons; but he found it impossible to retire despite his often professed intentions to give up work and live on the 1,100-acre Red Fox Farm about two miles south of Martin City in southwestern Jackson County, Missouri. Kemper accepted

appointment as chairman of the Missouri Social Security Commission, which administered old-age pensions, relief, and child-welfare programs in Missouri. Kemper, the railroad man, also spent the greater part of 1937 helping to reorganize the Missouri Pacific Railroad.

On Christmas Eve 1937, William Kemper, the physical enthusiast, underwent surgery at the University of Kansas Hospital. The seventy-two-year-old banker remained in the hospital until he died on January 19, 1938. Found in his billfold was a clipping someone had given to the banker that read: "'The final test of a gentleman,' says William Lyon Phelps, 'is his respect for those who can be of no possible service to him.'" The unidentified sender had penned an addendum: "You are doing it." The newspapers recounted the details, accomplishments, and the personal and business successes of the "ambidextrous handclasper" whose boyhood ambition had been to become a shoe manufacturer. The tributes left the clear impression that it would be difficult for anyone to follow in his footsteps.

One journalist looked at Kemper's life in larger terms. Sitting in his cluttered office in Emporia, Kansas, the nation's best-known newspaper editor sat down to write a different kind of tribute. William Allen White weaved his words carefully to eulogize one man's life and, in doing so, to reflect broadly on a nation's history.

"William T. Kemper was typically a successful American businessman with rather more spare energy and rather more intelligent emotional content than most businessmen. He touched life warmly and at many angles. But his success was as American as the flag. He began as a small townsman in Eastern Kansas. He found that his energies required a larger field. He went to Kansas City, began at the bottom, worked and saved, made friends, and earned money. He became a leading citizen by splicing the belt to his dynamo so that much of his surplus energy above money-making went into community service. As he went out of his forties into his fifties, he was a big man, not only for Kansas City, but for his region.

"He loved the Missouri valley. He could have gone to New York and been one of the national big fellows. But he did more good and was happier by staying in Kansas City. In the last 300 years in this country there have been 10,000 Kempers, all built on the same pattern—great diligence, indomitable purpose, broad imagination which is called vision when it is directed by wisdom, and upon an essential American kind heart. Upon men of this kind America has depended for her progress. They have been the bone and sinew of this land.

"And moreover, thank heaven, nothing has happened to America to keep her from repeating the Kemper pattern. We can still turn that trick, make Kempers little and big in every region, for years to come. Indeed, that very hope, based on the possibility of our country developing the energies of men so that they will build up the body and fabric of our country, is the thing that distinguishes America. This peculiar American quality is the solid basis of our country's high dream. Without that vision the people perish."

Hundreds gathered at Forest Hill Cemetery in south Kansas City when William Thornton Kemper was laid to rest. Standing near the front were Kempers "little and big" molded in the very "pattern" of the man they had come to remember. Banker Bill was dead; his sons would carry on.

until 1919 when a permanent home for the Federal Reserve Bank was completed on the opposite side of Grand Avenue. The R. A. Long Building also had housed commercial banks including Liberty National Bank, Liberty Trust Company, and, later, Columbia National Bank. Crosby could not have been happier: the downtown location was on Tenth Street with his two main competitors—First National Bank and Commerce Trust Company—yet it was the closest of the three to the Kansas City Federal Reserve Bank.

In February 1944, City National Bank announced that it had signed a fifteen-year lease, effective in May 1945, to use the first four floors of the R. A. Long Building. The bank also announced that it had spent $160,000 to purchase the adjoining five-story and four-story buildings directly north of the R. A. Long Building on Grand Avenue. The buildings were to be razed to permit the bank to construct an indoor parking garage. In the meantime, the bank continued to operate out of the cramped quarters at Eighteenth Street and Grand Avenue. The bank opened an international department under the direction of Swedish-born and educated Bror Unge and focussed much of its early efforts on business opportunities in Latin America. The bank, anticipating its move downtown, expanded its personnel by welcoming back servicemen. In 1941, bank employees numbered 109; but the staff had grown to 239 by the end of 1946.

Crosby was making a name in his own right in banking and busi-

ness circles. In a masterful 1944 performance befitting his father, Crosby had a major role in yet another memorable chapter over control of the Kansas City Southern. After wresting control of the Kansas City Southern in 1936, the rail line had been run by Charles P. Couch. He was considered a competent railroad man but was not firmly committed to running the railroad from the headquarters in Kansas City. A group headed by Crosby Kemper slowly began acquiring blocks of stock with the intention of gaining control of the Kansas City Southern; though they encountered difficulties because a large block of about 120,000 shares was owned by Dutch investors, whose proxies were vested with the Netherlands embassy in Washington, D.C.

In attempting to retain control of the Kansas City Southern, interests headed by Couch sought help from high-ranking government officials to pressure the Netherlands embassy to vote its proxies in favor of management. Kemper and his associates countered by making the behind-the-scenes maneuvering a public matter through the aid of political friends who called for a United States Senate investigation. The move demonstrated to Couch that Kemper and his associates were determined to gain control of the Kansas City Southern. When the 1944 annual meeting was held, Crosby's group named fifteen out of eighteen directors elected; and Couch conceded that the Kemper group was "sincere in its announced intention of removing control of the road to Kansas City" and had enough votes to do so.

Crosby's success in making the Kansas City Southern truly a Kansas City industry made doubters realize that the fifty-two-year-old banker was as formidable as his father. The Kempers had a well-earned reputation for running and building first-class banks, and now Crosby had found a prime downtown location for the little neighborhood bank that was growing into an important regional bank.

It took $2 million and two-and-a-half years before City National Bank and Trust—by then having grown to be Kansas City's third largest bank—moved eight blocks north on Grand Avenue to the R. A. Long Building. As a financial institution, the bank had come miles. In the nearly thirty years since the Kempers had taken over the bank in 1919, total deposits had increased by almost 250 percent in real dollars to $137.5 million in 1948, a remarkable financial story without parallel in Kansas City banking history. In its thirty-five-year history, the bank had expanded from a storefront bank with five employees to a major financial institution with $100-million-plus in deposits, 250 employees, and many correspondent banking relationships throughout the country and the world.

In moving downtown, City National Bank and Trust Company went first class. Marble, glass, and aluminum were used extensively in the bank lobby; but art and decor did not attract the greatest attention at the new bank. Crosby Kemper had a novel idea to build a Motor Bank as part of the bank's indoor parking garage. The bank touted its unique facility as the first of its kind in the country, but the Motor Bank actually was a better-marketed refinement of drive-in banking that had been developing within the banking industry for twenty years. In reality, the Motor Bank was an indoor park-

The new downtown lobby of City National Bank featured a $20,000 mural painted by Edward Laning, titled **Reunion at Kansas City,** *that depicted Indian and pioneer, cattleman and politician, slave and freeman as they visually converged at the confluence of the Missouri and Kaw rivers.*

and-walk banking facility. Customers drove into the indoor parking garage from Grand Avenue, walked into an enclosed air-conditioned room with four teller windows, transacted their business, and then departed without having to go into the main bank lobby. Crosby thought this arrangement preferable to having customers pull up to a drive-in window to conduct banking business from behind the wheels of their vehicles. He calculated that the walk-up windows could handle six times more customers during rush hour than a drive-in window.

The cold rain looked as if it might turn into snow when the newly uniformed guards opened the doors of the downtown City National Bank and Trust Company an hour-and-a-half early at 8 A.M. on Monday, November 10, 1947. The dark-haired head of the six-foot-two-inch Crosby was scarcely visible among the throngs of customers, friends, and out-of-

City National Bank considered its Motor Bank and indoor-parking garage a huge success. During 1952, the bank calculated that more than 225,000 cars had parked in the garage; and patrons had completed more than 160,000 transactions at the Motor Bank.

City National Bank demolished two buildings north of the R. A. Long Building to construct an indoor parking garage that incorporated a Motor Bank, an innovation of Crosby, Sr. Customers parked their cars and conducted their business at enclosed walk-up windows.

town bankers who came to congratulate the bank on its new facilities. Out-of-town bankers wandered through the bank's five floors, many stopping to take a long hard look at the bank's penthouse, which was intended for employees' use only and consisted of an eating counter where sandwiches, coffee, and soft drinks were served. On the roof was a sun deck with a shuffleboard and lounge chairs where employees could relax. Crosby and Kearney Wornall held court and greeted thousands of people by their first names as they strolled into the bank lobby. By day's end, Crosby had lost his voice, which made it difficult for him to speak that evening when 750 male guests of the bank gathered for a dinner at the Hotel Continental and about 300 women enjoyed a separate dinner at the Hotel Muehlebach.

The postwar period at the bank was a difficult time for women, many of whom had moved into positions that had been held almost exclusively by men prior to the war. Pendleton remembers that on the day the war ended, bank comptroller Edward Lyle invited all the department employees to his house for a picnic supper. "I remember sitting there and talking, and we all were coming from different viewpoints," she said. "The common philosophy was that the women had been holding the jobs until the men got back home, then the men would resume their jobs and the women would leave. But [Lyle] was very complimentary of the job that the women had been doing. He said 'I never thought we could do it but we did.'"

To his conservative competitors, Crosby's bold move downtown and his innovations marked him as a flamboyant banker in an industry that

The new Motor Bank located within the parking garage of City National Bank

In 1950, Charles Young, Jr. (left) was recruited by Crosby, Sr. (seated) to make some dramatic changes in the bank's trust department. Young was an attorney and had spent nearly ten years in banking in Kirksville, Missouri, before joining the prestigious Kansas City law firm of Warrick, Koontz and Hazard. He had been general counsel for the Saint Louis Federal Reserve Bank before joining City National Bank.

prided itself on its conservative practices. The innovations offered by the bank were services customers wanted. Aggressive marketing had been essential to the bank's success, and Crosby stated that his approach toward banking was based on "the theory of being conservative yet helpful."

One area in which the bank had been less than helpful was its trust department. The trust department, started in 1927, had been long considered a necessary bank service but had been scarcely a money-maker for the bank. Trusts were an adjunct to commercial banking and never had been regarded as very profitable. Crosby was quite upset when the attorney for Edgar Berkley, a long-time bank director, had First National Bank of Kansas City administer Berkley's estate because the attorney lacked confidence in City National's trust department.

Charles Young, Jr. changed all that. Intense and intelligent, Young already had established a reputation for himself in banking and legal circles when he was recruited by Crosby in 1950 to head City National Bank's trust department. Young brought energy and ideas to a complacent and staid banking department. City National Bank had been highly innovative in other banking services, but the fiduciary responsibility felt by the trust department discouraged it from looking at new business opportunities that trust management offered. Much of the trust work came in preparation of the legal documents, but the bank realized the fee income only when the individual died. Young had different ideas. "He conceptually understood

Your Responsibilities

1. To be constantly aware of the value of good public relations and conduct your public contacts accordingly.
2. To school yourself in the duties assigned to you so that your work assignment may be performed efficiently.
3. To prepare yourself for assuming greater responsibilities by home study and attendance at formalized classes.
4. To maintain a friendly attitude toward fellow employees and supervisors, thus gaining the greatest cooperation from others.
5. To be regular in attendance, prompt in reporting for work, and maintaining a neat, orderly appearance during business hours.
6. To prevent personal problems or business from interfering with your regular assigned duties during banking hours.

Our Responsibilities

1. To maintain the best working conditions possible to create a cheerful, pleasant atmosphere for performing work.
2. To offer opportunities for advancement for those capable of such advancement, by offering training and educational opportunties.
3. To keep our salary range equal to, or better than, other organizations in the same type of business enterprise.
4. To provide employee benefits such as vacations, sick leave, insurance and pensions.
5. To provide proper incentives for good work, and insofar as possible, to regard each individual as a distinct personality and not as "one of a group."
6. To provide lunchrooms, recreational facilities, and social activities consistent with the needs of the employees.

A trust agreement using the bank's forms developed by trust attorney Ruth Hall was sent to a Boston attorney handling a legal matter. The attorney was so impressed with the document that he wrote a complimentary letter to Charles Young saying he hazarded to guess that the document had been drafted by a Yale man. Young replied that the attorney was right as to the school, but wrong as to the sex.

the trust business as a dynamic instead of a static business, as a business to be marketed, where you had product development," explains Frank Terry, a bank trust officer who survived Young's temperamental tenure to later become head of the trust department.

Young changed City National Bank's whole approach toward its trust department. Young got bright Yale-educated attorney Ruth Hall to develop a book of legal forms that attorneys could use as model documents in setting up different kinds of trusts. The trust forms were readily received and highly regarded by the Kansas City legal community. The bank also published a probate code for Missouri, which pulled together under one cover all relevant state laws concerning trusts and estates. Attorneys eagerly requested extra copies from the trust department for their offices.

Equally as important was the new investment philosophy adopted by the trust department. Many trust departments, First National Bank of Kansas City included, concentrated trust-fund investments in government bonds because of their high security and liquidity. The test of law long had been whether the trustee, who had invested and managed assets for some beneficiary, had acted as a prudent man would have done in handling his own assets. Young knew trust law and knew it well but felt that the self-restraint of other trust-department investment policies was devised out of a primary consideration for avoiding lawsuits and was detrimental to earning a good rate of return. Aggressive investing never would have been permitted at most banks' trust departments, but Young had an agile intellect that allowed him to conceptualize without being constrained by past practices. However, legal training and banking experience made him prudent.

In February 1951, the bank established a common trust fund wherein small trusts could be pooled to permit greater diversification and more efficient management of the funds. The bank also began developing trust business from corporate accounts. Working with Hamilton Fund, Inc. of Denver, Colorado, the trust department in 1953 developed a profit-sharing retirement plan for the mutual fund. By developing a standardized plan, the trust department made it easy for other businesses to implement their own plans at a minimum cost. Between 1949 and 1954, the number of retirement plans administered by the trust department increased from two to forty-three. During that five-year period, the trust department personnel doubled, while the managed assets and earned revenues tripled.

Headquartered downtown and in a postwar boom, the bank continued to show tremendous growth. The customer base expanded as the number of deposit accounts more than doubled between 1942 and 1952, increasing from 22,463 accounts to 47,682. The bank passed two major milestones. In 1950, the bank's net earnings topped $1 million for the first time. Two years later, total bank deposits exceeded $200 million. The bank, in its annual reports, gloried in how it had grown in comparison to other Kansas City banks. The most startling comparison was for the twenty-year period between 1937 and 1957. Over the two decades, the deposits at City National Bank had increased from $20.8 million to $219.7 million, or a 955.2-percent increase. By comparison, deposits for all other Kansas City banks during the same period had increased from $366.1 million to $1.1 billion, a 209.6-percent increase. The growth thrilled the stockholders, none more so than the bank's biggest stockholder, Crosby Kemper.

The bank introduced other innovations as it tried to develop its personal-loan business. City National Bank became one of the first Kansas City banks to have a personal-loan department and one of the first in the country to offer loans on checking accounts for approved customers. The service was called Borrow by Check and was patterned after a plan developed by First National Bank in Boston. It allowed customers to establish a line of credit up to $1,200 in a special checking account. Whenever the customer needed money, he could write a check on the account up to the credit limit. Interest of 1 percent was charged on the previous month's outstanding loan balance, in addition to twenty-five cents for each check written.

The novel service attracted considerable attention and some controversy within the banking industry. One trade publication viewed the service as "an additional method of merchandising the installment credit and consumer loan department—another package to feature and sell, another way to get good names on the bank's books and keep them there." However, one Chicago banker considered the idea a questionable banking practice and wrote, "Historically, banks have urged people to borrow money only when they have a real need for funds, and to get out of debt as quickly as possible. Under this new plan, the debtor may be encouraged to stay in debt."

The Kempers' prominence in American banking was reflected in the 1954 election of Crosby, Sr. to the presidency of the 450-member Associ-

Crosby Kemper, Jr., about 1955

The Kempers were also gentlemen farmers who loved horses and owned country homes within driving distance of Kansas City. Crosby, Jr. had ridden polo ponies and chased the hounds, but above all loved the thrill of equestrian jumping, which he had learned at the Culver Military Academy in Culver, Indiana, during the summers of 1941, 1942, and 1943. The lanky youth and his horse—the Olympic jumper, American Lady—competed on the school's five-member exhibition team.

ation of Reserve City Bankers. Membership in the association was composed of the nation's largest banks in the twelve cities with Federal Reserve banks. Once one of the smaller Kansas City banks, City National had grown into one of the nation's larger banks, ranking 130th in size in 1955. The bank had ranked as high as 112th in 1950; but its ranking, as well as that of Commerce Trust, steadily dropped as larger banks developed in California, Texas, and the Pacific Northwest and as some states encouraged bank growth through branch banking.

The bank was continually hiring new employees as business grew steadily. In any situation, the dark-haired, six-foot-seven-inch handsome man in his mid-twenties would have attracted attention. He was personable, hard-working, intelligent, and ambitious; he would have been noticed even if his name had not been Rufus Crosby Kemper, Jr. The twenty-two-year-old Crosby, Jr. was hired by his father's bank in 1950.

Crosby, Jr. had spent two years in the United States Navy at the conclusion of World War II before enrolling at the University of Missouri. While at the university, he had considered foregoing the family banking business in favor of government service, perhaps the diplomatic corps; but the lure of banking had been stronger. Rather than traveling the world, his banking career began with a different kind of trip. "Dad put me in the night transit area, and I worked from seven o'clock in the evening until three in the morning meeting trains and sorting the checks," Crosby, Jr. said. Following six months of sorting checks by hand, the young Kemper moved out of the operations side of the bank and became an assistant cashier. He quickly advanced to assistant vice-president, then was made an executive vice-president in 1955, and was elected to the bank's board of directors in 1956.

Young Crosby, Jr.—the youngest of three children and the only son—had been liberally educated. He had attended Kansas City public schools; but when he had reached high-school age, his parents had sent the lanky youth to prestigious Phillips Academy in Andover, Massachusetts, a well-known preparatory school for the Ivy League. He had shown the athletic interests of the Kemper men and had participated in football, swimming, and equestrian jumping. He had towered over his peers, but his schoolmates and teachers had been impressed by more than his height. Using the slow and deliberate delivery that was typical of his midwestern background, Crosby, Jr. had developed into an excellent public speaker with an intellect that quickly mastered a subject and a resonant voice that pleased audiences. His talent had won the school's Carr Award for public speaking.

City National's success was largely a family affair. After gaining control of the bank, William Kemper and his son Crosby, Sr. had established a neighborhood base, improved services, and secured corporate accounts, which had created so much growth that the bank no longer was able to operate out of the building at Eighteenth Street and Grand Avenue. Now Crosby, Sr. and his son Crosby, Jr. would do the same at the downtown bank. There was one important difference: father and son looked upon City National Bank as their careers and had to work side by side, whereas William Kemper

Crosby Kemper, Jr. attends his first board of directors' meeting as the newly elected president of City National Bank in 1959.

had been only a major stockholder and not a full-time employee. The father-son business relationship of Crosby, Sr. and Jr. became more complicated and strained as the younger Crosby quickly moved up the corporate ladder. Crosby Kemper, Sr. had been twenty-seven years old when he had become president of the half-million-dollar City Center Bank in 1919; just a month short of his thirty-second birthday in 1959, his son became president of City National, which had $228 million in deposits. After forty years of being president of the bank, Crosby, Sr. was content to hold only the position of chairman of the board. Knowing that one day he probably would run the bank, Crosby, Jr. had worked in nearly every department so that he had acquired a hands-on, practical understanding of the bank, its policies, and its personnel. At the monthly board meetings, Crosby, Jr. was the only member under fifty years old and one of the few to have a full shock of hair. He commanded the respect of older community business leaders as he was outgoing, hard working, and practiced the Kemper philosophy of personal banking.

During the year prior to becoming bank president, Crosby, Jr. had been chairman of a newly organized executive committee that had given him broad overall control of bank operations. In that year, 1958, the bank had purchased for $2.5 million the fourteen-story R. A. Long Building where the bank had occupied four floors under a long-term lease. After the parking garage, Motor Bank, and annex had been added, the bank's cost for its headquarters had come to $4.6 million. The next year another banking innovation for pedestrians was initiated by construction of a 700-square-foot Patio Bank between the bank's two drive-in entrances on Grand Avenue.

Crosby, Jr. pushed for policy changes so that the bank concentrated more on developing the middle market and less on courting national accounts. The changes evolved partly out of having been turned away at the Federal Reserve discount window on one occasion when the bank desperately needed money for loan commitments that it had made to national customers. Crosby, Jr. realized that it was the middle-market customers who also were using the bank's bond and trust departments, while the national accounts wanted large sums of money at low interest rates and did little or no other business with the bank.

Other consequences, which shaped the character of the bank, flowed out of that shift in direction. The bank put less emphasis and resources into livestock and agricultural loans following the death of J. Milton Freeland in 1957 and made fewer international loans. Like a poker player, the bank played to its strengths—the bond and trust departments, which contributed significantly to the bank's overall financial strength. In 1951, fiduciary investments and miscellaneous income had amounted to $218,000, or 5.7 percent of the bank's gross income. By 1962, that figure had increased to $2.11 million or 17.6 percent. Interest on securities was $884,000, or 23.1 percent, in 1951 and stood at $2.87 million, or 24 percent, in 1962. The bond and trust departments also contributed to the bank's excellent industry reputation, and the bond department was a strong selling point when City National sought deposits and business from correspondent banks.

Although the Kemper father and son were alike in many ways, strong differences developed after Crosby, Jr.'s sudden decision to run for the United States Senate in 1962. The Kempers were not averse to politics; but Crosby, Jr. had the audacity to run as a Republican, a major transgression for the son of a prominent Democratic family. Father and son argued vehemently about the Senate race. Crosby, Sr. had spent forty years believing that there was no better job in the world than to be president of City National Bank. Now, after three years as his successor, his son could think of nothing more interesting, more important, or more rewarding than to run as a Republican for the United States Senate.

The Republicanism is what really hurt. Crosby, Sr. did not burn with the political passions of either his son or his own father William. Both Crosby, Sr. and his brother James had turned down personal requests from President Harry Truman to spearhead fund raising in western Missouri for the president's 1948 reelection campaign. Not only was Crosby, Jr. running

Mr. President, *(1967)*
lithograph, 14x11 in.,
Thomas Hart Benton

*"This is a conservative state,
and we have too many who are
Democrats because they hate
those Damn Yankees. The Civil
War was over 100 years ago. It
is time they wake up."*

Crosby Kemper, Jr., *1962*
United States Senate campaign

as a Republican, but he was quite young for a position that voters typically had bestowed upon battlewise, veteran politicians who were years older and substantially grayer than the youthful thirty-five-year-old banker.

Crosby, Jr. filed for his nominating petition more than a year before the November 1962 election and began crisscrossing the state. Invariably Kemper was asked why he was running as a Republican after having been treasurer of the Jackson County committee to reelect Democrat Stuart Symington to the United States Senate in 1958. The banker deftly replied, "I didn't leave the Democratic Party, the Democratic Party left me." Kemper

considered himself a political independent who held a strong conviction that the two-party system in Missouri needed to be revived. Politics gave the maverick in Crosby, Jr. full reign. With help of college friends, he ran his own campaign, spoke his own mind, and pulled few punches. "I am campaigning for what I believe in, so I don't need any polls. I am trying to appeal to people's higher instincts," he said. "They have them, you know."

Crosby, Jr.'s opponent in the general election was the stodgy, overweight fifty-four-year-old Edward Long, a Clarksville attorney and banker. Long had risen through the political ranks after being elected lieutenant governor for Missouri in 1954 and going to Washington when he won a 1960 special election to fill the unexpired term of Senator Thomas Hennings, who had died in office. The election results were surprising only in that Kemper fared much better than most expected. Long received 666,929 votes, 54.5 percent of the votes cast, compared to a total of 555,330 for Kemper. The Republican had run well in the rural areas but had lost the election primarily in the city of Saint Louis where there were allegations of Democratic voter fraud in black, inner-city precincts. Long was publicly discredited during his six-year term for using his office to shield Teamster president Jimmy Hoffa from serving a prison term for jury tampering. The Teamsters had pumped millions of dollars into Long's 1962 race against Kemper.

The election probably cost Crosby, Sr. a $10 bet with a former United States president. It had angered Harry Truman that a Kemper was seeking a major public office on the Republican ticket. Truman had become furious when he erroneously believed that the Kemper family and the bank were putting pressure on a Democratic lawyer to work in Kemper's campaign. Truman, acting on the incorrect information, penned a letter dated September 5, 1962, to Crosby, Sr. that showed the plain-speaking Truman at his most vindictive. Truman wrote: "Now I don't care a damn if one of the third generation of Kempers wants to go wrong because of the immense wealth of the family, but I do care if the second generation makes financial pressure a part of the campaign." Truman had been misinformed about the situation, but was prepared to use financial pressure to show how steamed he was. "I have some forty thousand dollars in one account in your bank," Truman wrote out in longhand. "I have twenty-five or thirty thousand in a [Truman] Library account and I have forty thousand in your brother's bank. Do you want me to do what you did to my young friend? I can cut you both off now and for the future if I want to." Having vented his anger, Truman decided not to send the letter after all and gave it to his secretary, who filed it away among the president's other papers.

Truman regularly got a haircut from Frank Spina, an Italian barber located at 110 West Tenth Street, who began cutting Truman's hair when the two served in Battery D of the 129th Field Artillery during World War I. Crosby, Sr. was striding up Tenth Street towards the bank late in the fall of 1962 when he noticed the former president getting his hair trimmed and went inside the barber shop to visit with Truman. With a general election just weeks away, the discussion naturally drifted into politics and culminated in a small wager. Exactly what the bet was about is unclear, but it may have been the Senate bid by Kemper's son because the bank president mailed

a short note to Truman following the election: "As usual you were right," Crosby, Sr. wrote. "Here is the ten dollars I bet you in the barber shop." Truman responded: "While I am happy to win the bet, I don't like to take the money of my good friends but I will put it to good use—maybe I will deposit it in the City National Bank, you never can tell!" Actually, Truman had close ties to City National Bank since he had named the bank as trustee of his estate. Truman also had set up trusts for his grandchildren, which were managed by the bank's trust department.

Following his election defeat, Crosby, Jr. devoted his full time and energy to the bank; but his father remained perturbed by his son's year-long political pursuits. The senior Kemper had assumed more responsibilities for day-to-day operations at the bank during the campaign, and father and son had problems deciding who was going to be in charge after the campaign was over. By 1963, the two vied over who would head the bank. The younger Kemper came to believe that his father was intentionally

trying to undermine Crosby, Jr.'s authority as bank president. Orders were countermanded when Crosby, Jr. was out of town, and the elder Kemper would challenge his son in front of other bank officers who were older employees loyal to Crosby, Sr. The younger Kemper was aggressive, impatient, and harder to work for than his father; though he was a good banker.

Crosby, Jr. wanted to be his own man, not his father's son. The big blowup occurred on a Friday. After harsh words were exchanged, Crosby, Jr. decided to resign and let his seventy-one-year-old father run the bank. Over the weekend, Crosby, Sr. had the furniture moved out of his son's first-floor office off the main lobby. The banking veteran took a certain amount of glee in his son's departure. He went over to John Hoffman, the bank's chief loan officer and long-time employee, and tapped him on the shoulder. "Well kid," Crosby, Sr. said, "we're back in business." In the newspaper, the typically candid Kempers were closemouthed. Crosby, Sr. said only that his son wanted "more time to devote to other interests," while wishing him well. It was a hard blow. Both loved banking, each cared for the other, but they were unable to resolve their differences. At thirty-six years of age, Crosby, Jr. was without a job after having resigned as president of one of the Midwest's largest banks. A friend wanted him to join a major bank in San Francisco, but he declined the offer. "I've got to do battle with the old man," Crosby, Jr. decided, "I've got to prove something to him and to me."

The proof stunned his father, who in other situations probably would have been quite proud of his son. Within two months of resigning his bank presidency, Crosby, Jr. had borrowed enough money to buy controlling interest in a small Kansas City bank, a bank that he could call his own and run as he saw fit. Young Crosby Kemper, Jr. had returned to the site of his father's early success at Eighteenth Street and Grand Avenue and had bought control of Grand Avenue Bank, which had opened in 1947 in the building formerly occupied by City National Bank before its move downtown. The Eighteenth and Grand location was the same building and the same neighborhood in which his grandfather and father had begun the task of building a first-class bank. This third-generation Kemper banker would do the same. He was willful, talented, determined, and driven by a desire to prove something to his father.

The plans Crosby, Jr. had for his new bank sounded like a page taken from his father's own career. "Many changes are in order for the Grand Avenue Bank," Crosby, Jr. said. "The first move will be to make it a full-service institution. Instead of a community bank, the management will seek to make it an area bank." Crosby, Jr. immediately announced plans to develop bond, trust, international, and correspondent banking departments. A story was about to repeat itself.

Life Magazine *believed that Crosby Kemper, Jr., at a height of 6 feet 7 inches, was the tallest candidate in the 1962 congressional races. This photograph of the gregarious candidate campaigning at a Kansas City shopping center appeared in its October 5, 1962, issue.*

Robert Kelley,
Life Magazine ©1962 Time Inc.

~6~

REACHING ACROSS A STATE

he whole situation was upsetting to Herbert Wilson. For more than fifteen years, he had sat at the directors' table of City National Bank and Trust and watched the bank grow into one of the state's great financial institutions. But in the past couple of years, he had found it difficult to attend the directors' meetings without regretting the 1963 rift that had prompted Crosby Kemper, Jr. to leave his father's bank and become president of Grand Avenue Bank. It was fitting, but sometimes awkward, that the younger Kemper had remained on the board of his father's bank. Several of the outside directors considered it unfortunate that the seventy-four-year-old father and his thirty-nine-year-old son had split because of differences over which of the two was to run the family-controlled bank.

Crosby, Jr. moved into the Grand Avenue Bank in March of 1964; and before long, the demanding younger Kemper—impatient and anxious to make his mark—clashed with the older Grand Avenue bank officers. Crosby, Jr. wanted to grow; they were happy being small. Within a few months of Crosby, Jr. having taken over Grand Avenue Bank, several of the top officers quit. One officer said he had already lived through one rat race with Crosby, Sr. and was not anxious to repeat the experience. Others eagerly welcomed a return to the Kemper style of banking, which had been practiced on the corner of Eighteenth and Grand until 1947 when City National Bank had moved downtown.

Crosby, Jr. immediately began remodeling the bank, recruiting his own officers, and promoting the bank in much the same way as his father had done forty years earlier. The bank invited speakers in, hosted large luncheons, and called on new accounts. Some companies that had done business with Crosby, Jr. at City National Bank moved some of their banking business to Grand Avenue Bank out of personal loyalty, which caused further friction between father and son. "Dad threatened people who did business with us," said Crosby, Jr. "It was quite a deal." The Grand Avenue Bank began moving, and between 1963 and 1966 deposits increased from $12.9 million to $21.5 million. Despite the impressive growth, Grand Avenue Bank was one of the smaller Kansas City banks and lacked the size, reputation, and clout of the $269-million City National Bank.

Crosby Kemper, Jr.

The Kempers had always believed in personal banking, promotions, and advertising years before reserved bankers considered it appropriate or effective for their conservative tastes.

Crosby, Jr. was turning Grand Avenue Bank around, but it was just too small for his ambitions. "A bank that size would take me a lifetime [to build] after being used to big banks," Kemper discovered. "After I'd turned it around and really got it going, I realized that it wasn't enough of a challenge, although I could have built it as time went on." Kemper felt that he had shown his father his true mettle with his modest success as president of a small bank. Had his father ever considered him to be a rich, indolent world traveler, his achievements at Grand Avenue Bank were ample refutation. The younger Kemper yearned to be back downtown, but the terms had to be different from those that had precipitated his departure.

About that time Wilson sought out Crosby, Jr. Through years of service on various community boards, the bank director had a well-earned reputation for reconciling differences between powerful community leaders and interests by working behind the scenes. Wilson, who was president of Emery, Bird, Thayer department store, enjoyed a good relationship with both Kempers. All three men had worked together as bank directors and in several community organizations, including the Chamber of Commerce, the Starlight Theater Association, the American Red Cross, the Boy Scouts, and the American Royal. Wilson thought it had been very unfortunate that Crosby, Jr. and his father had split and proposed that the two men consider a reconciliation for the good of their personal relationship and the bank.

With his son's departure from the bank, Crosby, Sr. had resumed the dual title of chairman of the board and president of the bank. By the next year, Charles Young had become bank president. Young had years of banking experience, but it was almost solely concerned with trust matters and related legal issues. He never had worked in commercial lending or had extensive experience on the operations side of banking. Big banks, in general, were becoming more complicated to run and were undergoing a difficult transition to computerization.

In April 1959, the American Bankers Association had approved industry standards that permitted checks to be magnetically encoded with routing and account numbers so that they could be electronically sorted. City National Bank recognized the future and embraced the new computer technology more readily than other banking institutions, largely because of the bank's extensive involvement in managing investment trusts that had hundreds of thousands of individual accounts. "Automation in banks, just as in industry, is the key to stabilizing some of our costs and to . . . rapid and accurate processing of data," the bank stated. In 1961, City National Bank added another floor above the parking garage to house the computer operations. The IBM computers, installed in July 1962, were the first electronic computers to be used in a commercial bank in Kansas City. The bank also was the first institution in the Tenth Federal Reserve District to establish electronic fund transfers with the Kansas City Federal Reserve Bank. By 1965, programmers at City National Bank had written more than 400 computer programs for their IBM system. The bank supported its own computer operations by offering computer services, including electronic data processing

Keeping watch over the bank's electronic data-processing equipment was a growing cadre of employees that had grown from fifteen to nearly one hundred in only a few short years.

and payroll accounting, to outside businesses and to its correspondent banks on a fee basis.

Computerization helped to strengthen the bank's trust department and provided another valuable service to correspondent banks that could not afford the equipment and personnel for their own computer operations. City National Bank continued to grow; but the bank had begun moving in a major new direction by approving large real-estate loans, some for large-scale projects outside the state. Crosby, Jr., though no longer in charge, still felt strongly that the bank was drifting away from the middle market of Kansas City and regional businesses that he had considered so essential to the bank's continuing health and long-term growth. "Dad wanted to show me up and he made these real-estate construction loans; [the bank] made them all over the country," said the younger Kemper. When problems developed with some of the real-estate loans, Young and other key officers decided that the bank was becoming too big for any one person to handle. If Crosby, Jr. were convinced to return, Young could concentrate his energies on the bond and trust departments and leave commercial lending to the more experienced younger Kemper.

Crosby, Jr. had proven himself at Grand Avenue Bank, but he had missed the challenges of City National Bank and had been concerned about developments there. Unless he returned, City National Bank would cease to be a family institution since he was the only son in the family and neither of his two older sisters had been raised to work in the male-dominated banking world. The expectations that Crosby, Jr. would one day run his father's bank had been there from that day—February 22, 1927—when a boy had been born to Enid and Crosby Kemper. "I was six years old when I started learning the banking business," said Crosby, Jr. "At that age I was listening to my father and talking with my grandfather. One of the first things I heard from my father is that it doesn't do any good to say, 'the other banks are doing it, too,' if you're just as broke as they are."

A firm nudge from Wilson encouraged the two strong-willed Kempers to work out their differences. In August 1966, the bank announced that Crosby Kemper, Jr. was returning to his old post as president of City National Bank; Young was to become vice-chairman of the board; and Crosby, Sr. was retiring from active participation in the bank.

On his first day back, Crosby Kemper, Jr. was called into his old first-floor office by Crosby, Sr., who had occupied it during Crosby Jr.'s absence. A promise was made that partly healed the hurtful words the two had exchanged two-and-a-half years earlier. The father looked at his prodigal son and said, "I'll move upstairs, and I'll really get out this time." From that day on, the elder Kemper refrained from attending the bank's annual meetings or actively involving himself in the bank's affairs. If any doubt remained about who was managing the bank, it was clearly resolved the following year when Crosby, Sr. announced his retirement almost a year to the day after his son had returned to the downtown bank.

The senior Crosby Kemper marveled at how he had borrowed

$25,000 in order to buy 20 percent of the stock in the little City Center Bank back in 1919. "I still have the same stock," Crosby, Sr. said. "We are probably the only bank in the nation that has earned virtually all of its own capital. Most fellows in my position don't have enough stock to keep from getting pushed out when they get to be sixty-five." Crosby, Sr. still owned a fifth of his bank; he had succeeded in turning the $25,000 loan into millions. What Crosby, Sr. said about his customers was equally true of his own business career in banking: "You make a loan to some fellow with character who has a good idea and wants to work at it. You watch while through his efforts and abilities—and your money—he develops a very large business. That is one of the finest rewards in banking."

The bank that once had been run by five employees out of a one-story brick building now had 700 employees operating out of a steel-frame downtown skyscraper. Since Crosby, Sr. had been bank president, total deposits had increased from $600,000 in 1919 to $397 million in 1967. Crosby,

Sr. had remained busy building his bank and had avoided the ignominy of being forced to retire as his father had been from Commerce Trust Company, not once but twice. Crosby, Jr. took over the main first-floor office and maintained an open door, just as his father and grandfather had done.

Though both Kempers believed in personal banking, they did differ significantly on certain key banking issues. The elder Kemper believed in buying long-term bonds, while Crosby, Jr. believed in buying bonds short and maintaining bank liquidity. Though he had been an innovative banker, Crosby, Sr. opposed bank-issued credit cards, believing that banks which did issue credit cards were "pretty much like sheep" being led to financial slaughter. Crosby, Jr., on the other hand, believed that full-service banking meant being able to offer a widely accepted credit card to customers. In 1968, Crosby, Jr. and several other Kansas City bankers investigated whether to issue their own multibank, all-purpose credit card or to align with an existing card. In May 1969, City National Bank, First National, and Commercial National Bank in Kansas City, Kansas, began issuing Bankmark credit cards, a regional credit-card system that later merged with other regional card issuers to become the MasterCharge system.

*B*ack in command at City National Bank, Crosby, Jr. helped to mold a new approach that became critical to the bank's long-term growth and profitability. He did not want to become a money-center bank for the region and engage in massive money brokering. Confident and sure in his own judgment, Kemper was uneasiest when his bank was participating with some other institution to make a loan and was not the lead bank. He tried to prevent his bank from being "victimized by someone else's bad judgment" and wanted City National to call the shots in any major deal. His attitude effectively kept the bank from participating in loans to Fortune 500 companies and the high-risk energy field and concentrated City National Bank's efforts in the middle market of smaller midwestern companies.

Corporate treasurers, looking for the lowest interest rates, contacted the money-center banks across the country. A money-center bank often did not have enough deposits on hand to make the loan but would issue a loan commitment that it fulfilled by purchasing surplus funds from other banks across the country. Often only a razor-thin interest differential existed between the rate paid by the money-center bank to get the surplus funds and the rate it charged the customer in interest. Kemper felt uneasy about City National purchasing other banks' surplus funds in order to make loans to companies outside the region. The bank was more interested in quality loans than in quantity, and it made loans from money that customers had deposited with the bank. Even when City National Bank sold surplus funds to other banks, Crosby, Jr. wanted to be certain that the bank seeking funds was sound and not purchasing funds to infuse blood into a sick bank.

The bank enjoyed an almost nonpareil reputation among midwestern bankers. City National's strengths were obvious: strong trust and bond departments, electronic data processing, close proximity to the Kansas City Federal Reserve Bank, and strong management headed by ownership with

Glen E. Densmore, Jr., assistant vice-president, and R. Crosby Kemper, Sr. discuss computer technology in the bank's data-processing department, at the time located on the sixth floor over the parking garage.

For four decades, City National Bank and Trust Company used **The Scout** *as its corporate symbol. The trademark was abandoned when the bank holding company expanded statewide.*

In 1958, Missouri voters rejected a measure to permit branch banking. The highly emotional issue failed to pass in a single county. One radio ad featured a screaming woman who controlled her hysteria long enough to blurt out that she was being chased by "The Branch Bank Monster."

a controlling interest. The trust department had grown quickly from a department of thirteen employees in 1952 to 184 employees in 1967. The services that City National Bank performed for the rapidly growing field of mutual funds contributed greatly to the department's growth. The bank provided a variety of services, including shareholder accounting, being custodian of fund assets, and acting as an agent by handling transfers, dividends, proxies, and share redemptions. The bank was constantly upgrading and adding to its computer operations and by 1969 was one of the first banks to offer on-line data access to its mutual-fund customers. "There was a time when the mutual-fund industry used the large East Coast banks almost exclusively for shareholder servicing," Charles Young, Jr. explained. "We recognized this market potential and devoted extensive research to the development of systems capable of providing these various services at both a competitive and profitable price."

City National Bank successfully took advantage of opportunities in the changing financial market, even as the Missouri banks faced the most fundamental institutional change since the Great Depression. Since 1899, Missouri had been a unit-banking state, which restricted even the

United Missouri Bank of
Kirkwood, Missouri

*"We'd decided which banks we
wanted to visit ahead of time;
and we just walked in, sat
down, and visited with them.
We told them what our goals
were and what we could offer
them. We got the verbal okay,
came back, drew up the agreements, and mailed the papers
to them."*

John Kramer, *vice-president
correspondent banking,
December 1969*

largest banking institutions to conducting business from a single location,
although later legislative changes permitted a separate drive-in facility. Repeated efforts to initiate branch banking in Missouri had been soundly
defeated by the vociferous opposition of the more numerous small, independent bankers. The unit-banking rule effectively stunted growth at Missouri's
larger banks, and downtown banks found it increasingly difficult to compete for deposits as the growing number of suburbanites opted in favor of
banking with convenient neighborhood banks.

Faced with strong opposition to modifying the unit-banking law,
big city banks found an alternate means to extend their reach and their operations by forming bank holding companies—a legal device that permitted
de facto branch banking. A bank holding company provided a legal umbrella
under which a number of Missouri banks could be affiliated into a statewide
banking network, though the individual institutions still would be under the
control of local bank directors and management. An acquisition that would
result in restricted banking competition within a community could be rejected by federal banking agencies.

The move to form bank holding companies was led by Commerce
Trust Company, which formed its own holding company in February 1967
and acquired banks in Springfield, Joplin, and Brunswick. That summer,

"Corporate art collecting is not new, but it has changed dramatically. In the early days the practice was limited to displaying time-honored reproductions and corporate heirlooms, like an original Coleman's Mustard poster, portraits of founding fathers, or perhaps even a company's first left-hand screw that for generations controlled the pressure in the building's steam boilers."

United Missouri Bancshares
1973 Annual Report.

Although Crosby, Jr. purchased many art pieces through private dealers or at auctions, he also commissioned larger works—particularly sculptures that reflected more modern tastes—for display in bank lobbies. His selection of paintings favored realism and figurative art because those works retained their investment value and were more readily appreciated by bank customers. Just as in other aspects of business, the bank had a commitment to first-class original art.

Cream Surf,
oil, 13x19 in.,
George Bellows

City National Bank did the legal work to form its own holding company called Citibanc Shares of Missouri, Inc. The plan was shelved on Young's advice to avoid some potentially adverse tax consequences because of the Kempers' ownership position. Further work resolved any potential problems, and the bank in 1969 received approval from its stockholders, the Comptroller of the Currency, and the Federal Reserve to form a one-bank holding company that was named Missouri Bancshares, Inc. Stock in City National Bank was converted into stock in the holding company, which now owned the state's fifth largest bank. Within months, the one-bank holding company moved to become a registered multibank holding company in order to acquire other banks.

In December 1969, Crosby, Jr. and John Kramer, a vice-president in correspondent banking, drove to southwest Missouri to look for banks interested in being acquired. "We just hopped in the car," said Kramer, "and we knew all the bankers from being in the correspondent bank area. We knew them by first name, and we knew all about the banks." During their week-long trip, Crosby Jr. and Kramer worked out tentative agreements with four out of the five banks they visited.

The first banks to be acquired by Missouri Bancshares, Inc. were Kemper State Bank in Boonville, Central National Bank of Carthage, Security National Bank of Joplin, and Peoples National Bank of Warrensburg. All the banks had competitors in their communities and, with the exception of Kemper State Bank, all had national charters. As of December 1969, the four banks had collective total deposits of $62.5 million and more than a hundred employees. The acquisitions, along with the steady growth of City National Bank, pushed the total deposits of the holding company up to $492.7 million, just shy of a half-billion dollars, at the end of 1970. The acquisitions made Missouri Bancshares the state's fourth-largest banking concern. Many bank holding companies, bolstered by growth, rewarded their top executives with increased perks. Missouri Bancshares was not one of them. "We never had airplanes or chauffeurs," said Kramer. "We didn't have fancy cars. We operated without those privileges."

Crosby, Jr. and Kramer, coming off their successful winter bank-hunting trip, turned their attention to other prey, hoping to bag a big bank in Saint Louis. Crosby, Jr. contemplated a strategic merger that would quickly vault Missouri Bancshares into a powerful banking organization with a strong presence in Saint Louis and thought the Saint Louis suburban banks held by Mark Twain Bancshares could be acquired. The banks had been built from scratch by Adam Aronson, who left a large photo-supply business to go into banking. The two bankers were similar in many ways: both men appreciated modern art, liked running their own show, possessed strong personalities, and had achieved tremendous growth over a sustained period.

Aronson and Crosby, Jr. got together in Brookfield to discuss a merger during a directors' meeting of the Brookfield Banking Company, a northern Missouri bank in which Crosby, Jr. had bought a controlling interest in 1958. They proposed a marriage, but were unable to agree on the

Girl in a Landscape, *(1965)*
oil, 45½x44 in.,
Fairfield Porter

The Garden Bank, Fourteenth Street and Grand Avenue, Kansas City, Missouri

and pencil something out. He likes you to hand it to him. You give him a one-page memorandum, and he'll pick it up pretty quickly."

Crosby, Jr. surrounded himself with people he trusted, demanded much of them, and then helped to shape the banking policies and practices that he expected them to implement. Among those Crosby, Jr. brought into the bank was Jerome Scott, Jr., a Kansas City automobile dealer who made a mid-life career change to banking in 1967. Intellectually, Scott operated on the same level as Crosby, Jr. He was urbane and interested in theater, yet was well grounded in business.

Scott represented a younger generation of leadership, men that Crosby, Jr. had pulled into the bank. Crosby, Jr. and Charlie Young, as the years went by, increasingly had differed over how the bank was going to be

Lake Tahoe,
oil, 18x22 in.,
John Young-Hunter

run and who was going to be in charge. The inevitable clash put Crosby, Sr. in the unenviable position of having to choose between his son and his highly valued trust man. "I pretty well ran the bank," said Crosby, Jr., "and Charlie came to resent that. I didn't think he knew much about lending or public relations. He was a good trust man, but he had the determination to be boss. He went to my father; and, of course, my father supported me." Ongoing conflicts with Crosby, Jr. prompted the fifty-five-year-old Young to take early retirement in December 1971 to become president of Texas Bank and Trust Company in Dallas. Scott, who had been with the bank only four years, was made president of United Missouri Bank of Kansas City.

One problem confronting the Kansas City bank as it expanded into a holding company was a lack of space. The bank was running out of room in the fourteen-story R. A. Long Building; and it needed more room for its growing trust department, computer operations, and support personnel for

the holding company. The bank's space problems were partially resolved when it paid $1 million in December 1967 for the Kansas City Title Insurance Company Building located on the corner of Tenth and Walnut and contiguous to the main bank. Through extensive remodeling, the bank building and the title company building were connected to allow interior access between the two buildings.

As they had begun to lose customers to suburban facilities, downtown banks had placed new emphasis on customer service. City National Bank had done so with its innovative Motor Bank and its walk-up Patio Bank, an alcove on Grand Avenue between Ninth and Tenth streets where customers could bank. In late 1960, the bank had acquired property in the 1400 block of Grand and McGee for construction of a Garden Bank, so named because of the unusual landscaping around the banking facility. Another consideration in acquiring the site had been its proximity to the interstate highway that was under construction. Over the years, the bank had continued to acquire parcels of land in the neighborhood until it virtually owned the entire two-block area between Fourteenth and Fifteenth streets, McGee and Walnut.

Since the bank was about to outgrow its headquarters, bank officers were investigating new building plans. When the bank had purchased the title company building in 1967, it had announced that it was considering erecting a new eighteen-story bank building at Tenth and Walnut; but that plan also had been displaced by yet another, bolder move, completely unexpected in its size and scope.

*D*owntown Kansas City suffered the same malady facing other American urban centers—the "transformation from a vital marketplace of commerce and culture into a nine-to-five, weekday office and government center." The major banks were committed to downtown because the Federal Reserve Bank was so central to much of their important correspondent banking work. Bankers believed revitalization of downtown was important in order to protect their own property, increase retail trade, and maintain an urban center. Civic pride was involved; great cities, they believed, had great downtown areas; and Kansas City was looking rather shabby.

There had been one notable downtown development. In 1965, Commerce Trust Company, headed by James Kemper, Jr., had constructed a thirty-story office building adjoining its bank building. It was, at the time, the tallest commercial building in the state of Missouri and a harbinger of better things to come to downtown Kansas City. Crosby, Jr. anxiously wanted his bank to make a major impact on downtown redevelopment and quietly had been considering the possibilities. He had his eye on the property located just a block south of City National Bank on the half-block of Grand and Walnut facing Eleventh Street, better known as Petticoat Lane. Urban planners considered the site of the former Emery, Bird, Thayer department store a key parcel for redeveloping downtown.

Crosby, Jr., who steadily had increased his personal investment in downtown Kansas City real estate over a fifteen-year period, bought the

"This is how great cities are built. Ideas are thrown out and men grasp them and run with the ball . . . An imaginative development of the land seems a foregone conclusion because of the high cost of acquisition. There is no economic way the property can be cleared and used for surface parking or some other secondary use, a fate shared by many prominent downtown locations. It is reasonable to assume that Kemper would not have made this type of commitment without an ambitious scheme in mind."

Kansas City Times *editorial,* January 30, 1971

Solemn Pledge, *(1937)*
pastel, 18½x18½ in.,
Walter Ufer

Emery, Bird, Thayer property from the owner, Auto Lec Stores, Inc. of New York. Publicly, Crosby, Jr. remained indefinite about his plans when he announced in January 1971 that he had bought the site. "Because of my belief in the future of Kansas City and the conviction that the future of the city emanates from the core area, I decided to buy the property for future improvement," the banker said; but within a week, he announced that City

National Bank would construct a new headquarters and raze the department store. He had invited five very prominent national architects to Kansas City to develop preliminary sketches for a new bank headquarters. Then, in late February 1971, Crosby, Jr. announced that the bank had retained I. M. Pei and Partners of New York to design a ten-story building with 500,000 square feet of space, of which the bank would use about 120,000 square feet as a headquarters for its growing holding company.

The bank had retained an architect with an international reputation for designing buildings that sparked new life into downtowns by making the structures something other than nine-to-five centers. The Chinese-born American architect Ieoh Ming Pei set out to design a structure that would "become an oasis in downtown, a garden in the center." Crosby, Jr. and Pei failed to anticipate that creating the oasis would result in a conflict between aesthetics and economics. The bank structure was to be the city's first major building project since the construction industry had been plagued by major union strikes, an added complication to a national economy already deep in the throes of a serious recession. Crosby, Jr. wanted assurances that there would be a period of "labor peace and productive work." Another economic factor became involved: the headquarters building was planned to house the bank's holding company, but acquisition of affiliate banks was absorbing much of the company's surplus capital that otherwise might have been applied to the costs of building the headquarters. High interest rates, labor problems, new demands for capital, an imaginative architect accustomed to deep-pocketed clients, and a banker who was uneasy about constructing speculative office space created complications for the project that would take a decade to resolve.

An athletic man, Crosby, Sr. had enjoyed good health throughout his life but often ignored signs of any medical problem. A fanatical college-football fan, the former Missouri tackle—called "The Bear" by teammates—went to Lincoln, Nebraska, for the weekend of October 21, 1972, to see the Missouri–Nebraska football game. It was a pleasant enough weekend; but after returning home late Sunday night, the banker felt chest pains and asked his wife Enid to take him to Saint Luke's Hospital in Kansas City. The eighty-year-old banker died the next afternoon from an aneurysm.

Crosby, Sr. had loved banking and had mastered its complexities in a way that his father William would have found difficult. Banking had become more regulated, more automated, and more competitive since the days when William Kemper had made his mark as a banker, politician, and railroad man. Both men exemplified an approach to banking—personal contacts, aggressive marketing, community involvement, and ownership control—that had distinguished them as bankers and community leaders.

For certain, he had borne the family name; but Crosby, Sr. had also repeated "the Kemper pattern" that William Allen White had praised when William Kemper had died thirty-four years earlier. Another Kemper cut from the same pattern stood in line: Crosby, Jr. would carry on.

~7~

R. Crosby Kemper, Jr.

MAKING A DIFFERENCE

Only four days had elapsed since the death of R. Crosby Kemper, Sr. The stonemasons were still carving the banker's simple red-granite headstone when his son Crosby, Jr. made a dramatic announcement: the Kemper family was going to contribute $1.5 million to the American Royal Association in memory of his father for construction of a new arena in the stockyards. "He always thought agriculture was the basis of our city and that it should be supported," the son said.

The American Royal gift included contributions of family members but came primarily from the Enid and Crosby Kemper Charitable Trust, which the banker had established through his will. Crosby, Sr. had left the bulk of his private wealth to a charitable trust with the stipulation that his son and other trustees were to have wide discretion over how the money was to be allocated for the public good. As a trustee, Crosby, Jr. was to make the trust a highly visible and effective means for promoting the arts, building a downtown hotel, and preserving the American Royal. The gift to the American Royal marked the beginning of a singularly important chapter in the history of Kansas City philanthropy.

In the decade following his father's death, Crosby Kemper, Jr. molded United Missouri Bancshares into a highly profitable, statewide banking organization while simultaneously exerting wide-ranging influence and decisive leadership in Kansas City civic affairs. Having access to money and being a formidable fundraiser made Kemper a financial savior for more than one seemingly doomed-to-failure project, including the Vista Hotel and the Kansas City Symphony. His independent style of leadership earned Crosby, Jr. praise and excoriating criticism and made him more controversial than his father, who had not been as quick to express his viewpoint at public forums. A seasoned campaigner, Crosby, Jr. was more willing to step up and publicly speak his mind; and now he could do so without fear of losing votes. He cared deeply about his community and took personal offense when he thought he had been unjustly criticized in the press or privately for doing what he had considered best for the community.

As members of Kansas City's dominant banking family, the two Kemper cousins—James, Jr. at Commerce Trust Company and Crosby, Jr. at

Annie, *(1985)*
watercolor, *30x21½ in.,*
Doug Brega

United Missouri Bank—were relied upon by the business community to provide a lion's share of financial and community leadership; but a number of self-styled critics in the community felt that what the Kempers did was "not enough," "too much," and, rarely, "just right." A typical example was a little rift over building a downtown sports arena in 1971. Jackson County Presiding Judge George Lehr, an elected administrative official, tore into the

banking family: "The Kemper family in this town has stampeded the downtown interests as well as many other interests into inaction for years. And I think we're at a critical point as to whether the Kempers are going to control this city or whether new progressive leadership will emerge."

*J*udge Lehr's comment prompted William Kemper, Jr.—the youngest son of William Kemper—to write a personal letter back to the politician informing the community "newcomer" that "inaction" most definitely was not the appropriate adjective to describe the Kemper family's business or community efforts. "I must tell you," William, Jr. wrote, "that the family has given anonymously to individuals, to businesses, and to cultural institutions and many other projects which would never have been sparked had it not been for the modest manner in which we tried to do these things. . . . We have never tried to live off the taxpayers, but have tried to be honest, progressive, and constructive citizens. . . ."

With the 1972 gift to the American Royal, Crosby Kemper, Jr. pushed the family's philanthropic efforts onto the front pages of the newspapers. One motivation was public recognition for his father, whose private wealth had funded the trust. The family considered the initial charitable-trust gift to be a fitting memorial to the deceased banker, as he and his family had been among the preeminent supporters of the American Royal.

Kansas City and the agricultural exposition had a long history dating back to 1899 when a tent had been set up in the stockyards for a Hereford Fat Stock Show to exhibit 500 head. Within two years, the show had been expanded to include other breeds and the name had been changed to the American Royal. Later, a horse show had been added. Many community leaders had viewed the American Royal with indifference, if not disdain, as an event that had continued to promote a persistent image of Kansas City as a cow town populated by rural hicks and country bumpkins. To Crosby, Jr., the stockyards represented the symbolic and historic heart of the city. The city's two early industries—meatpacking and rail transportation—were attributed directly to Kansas City having been the business center for the great agricultural heartland. Crosby, Jr. wanted to save the American Royal despite the long-standing desires of others to see the agricultural fair sink into oblivion. Crosby, Jr. and his father had served on the American Royal board of governors and had been organization officers.

The Kemper gift provided the impetus for political and business leaders to put together a complicated financial package of $20.3 million that included general obligation bonds, revenue bonds, and private funds. When the project needed additional money, Crosby, Jr. increased the family's initial charitable gift to $3.2 million and recommitted the funds when the project nearly collapsed because of dissension concerning the location of the all-purpose arena. In recognition of the family's influential role, the Kansas City Council decided that the 18,000-seat facility should be named the R. Crosby Kemper Memorial Arena. United States Secretary of Agriculture Earl Butz was the guest speaker when the new arena was dedicated on October 14, 1974. Crosby, Jr. took the occasion to remind the city of its strong agricultural

Sisters 1985,
watercolor, *30x21½ in*
Doug Brega

Crosby, Jr. began art collecting as a student at the University of Missouri–Columbia. The young collegian paid $500 each for two portraits by the great Missouri artist George Caleb Bingham of pioneer steamboat captain Joseph Kinney and Matilda Kinney. He purchased the paintings at a sale at Rivercene, a grand mansion near Boonville, Missouri, that overlooked the Missouri River and had been owned by the steamship captain.

ties. "People out of New York come here and they tell us we ought to forget our cow-town image, that it is no longer an asset, that it's bad for our image," the banker said. "That's a lot of bunk. Agriculture is our greatest asset; and we should rededicate ourselves to that industry that provides this community, in one way or another, with 80 percent of its income."

Crosby, Jr.'s interests also included a life-long love for the visual and performing arts. Within six months of contracts having been let for the arena, Crosby, Jr. announced a second major gift of $5 million for a performing-arts center on the campus of the University of Missouri–Kansas City. The gift, at the time, was the largest single private donation in the history of the university system; and UMKC intended to name the $16-million facility the Enid Jackson Kemper Center for the Performing Arts in honor of the banker's seventy-six-year-old mother, who was still living at the time and

United Missouri Bancshares and the Kemper-related foundations have provided significant financial support to cultural institutions throughout the state. The Enid and Crosby Kemper Charitable Trust acquired Thespian Hall (right) in Boonville, Missouri, and made a gift of the four-story building to the Friends of Historic Boonville. The hall, originally built in 1857 in Greek-revival style of architecture, is included in the National Register of Historic Places and is a cultural center for the community. The Kemper foundation also has helped to fund the Kansas City Lyric Opera, which stages major operatic productions such as Giuseppe Verdi's classic grand opera, **Tosca** *(left).*

had been extremely supportive of the arts since moving to Kansas City following her 1921 marriage to Crosby Kemper, Sr.

The project eventually did transform the urban university campus, but not before it had severely tested the goodwill of Crosby, Jr. and the other trustees of the charitable trust. With the commitment of the substantial Kemper gift, the scope of the project was enlarged to include the school's Conservatory of Music. Construction could not begin, though, without a $6.4-million appropriation from the Missouri Legislature, which supposedly was forthcoming. Delays in funding the expanded project resulted in a higher price tag because of escalation in construction costs. Two years after announcing the $5 million grant, Kemper withdrew the challenge gift when the lowest construction bid came in at $2.7 million over the original project estimate. Private fund-raising efforts had been unable to make up the difference. Rather than having been a guardian angel of the arts, Crosby, Jr. emerged from the episode as the despicable devil, and it remained a sore

Into Deep Snow,
oil, 16x20 in.,
James Butler

point for years to come. "They only asked for $3 million; and I committed $5 million, just to make sure they had enough money to get the job done right," Crosby, Jr. said. "They kept messing around with it year after year, and the cost kept going up. Finally, I said we couldn't withhold the income any longer because the trust had to spend its income; and they would have to come to some kind of a decision."

The decision to withdraw the Kemper gift for the university performing-arts center came on the heels of a more painful decision earlier in January of 1975 to permanently table construction of the I. M. Pei–designed downtown headquarters that was to have been called the United Missouri Bank Plaza. Economic conditions made Crosby, Jr. uneasy about future developments. In his 1974 economic appraisal, the Kansas City banker worried about the recently imposed wage-and-price controls, prospects of a 25-percent annual inflation rate, and growing deficits. "We must not have the fear of controls over our heads, as just the mere thought of controls provokes higher prices," the banker said.

The bank never had built speculative office space. The seven-story bank building at Eighteenth Street and Grand Avenue had been fully rented when the building had opened in 1927. The bank had moved into leased space in the R. A. Long Building in 1947 and in 1958 had purchased the fourteen-story building when bank growth had necessitated expansion. In 1967, the bank had purchased the Kansas City Title Insurance Company Building because it needed more room. However, the Pei design for the bank headquarters had envisioned a 500,000-square-foot building with twin ten-story triangular towers that would have provided three times the square footage of the R. A. Long Building. The bank would have needed only a fraction of the available space in the headquarters; and leasing commitments to fill the upper floors in the two proposed towers were difficult to secure, partly because of the economic recession.

Downtown interests, enthusiastic about the prospects of an impressive new building in the once-thriving downtown business district, had been disappointed with delays in starting construction and were even more unhappy when the project was permanently tabled by the bank. Crosby, Jr. and the bank management were unconvinced that the Pei-designed bank headquarters would be beneficial to the bank's stockholders. They were more persuaded by the view that constructing the downtown edifice would be a long-term burden on bank earnings because office rentals would not cover the cost of the two ten-story triangular towers that were essential elements in Pei's design. Ten years later, Crosby, Jr. continued to show his aversion to "speculative building" without signed leases from major tenants. In a 1985 speech to real-estate developers, Crosby, Jr. said that overbuilding by office developers would create a "blood bath" leading to foreclosures, bankruptcies, and problem loans for banks. "I'm glad it's all being built; I'm just glad I don't have the mortgages on it," Crosby, Jr. said.

United Missouri Bancshares was not opposed to making major expenditures for brick and mortar, but it did so to meet existing banking needs.

The Park Bank in Saint Joseph, Missouri, which became United Missouri Bank of Saint Joseph after it was acquired in 1976.

Many of the holding company's newly acquired banks needed new buildings, extensive remodeling, or drive-in facilities. Between 1973 and 1976, United Missouri Bancshares had acquired nine new banks. Major acquisitions secured banks in Saint Joseph and Springfield, two of the state's more populous cities: the seven-year-old First City Bank of Springfield was acquired in 1974, followed by the acquisition of Park Bank in Saint Joseph in 1976. Two more banks were located in rural communities: First National Bank of Milan and Gillioz Bank and Trust Company in Monett. Two other banks were acquired in the Kansas City area: Wornall Bank and Hickman Mills Bank and Trust Company. United Missouri Bancshares also obtained new charters for three other banks in Saint Louis, Jefferson City, and Blue Springs, which involved court suits, regulatory hearings, and years of work. Downtown Saint Louis bankers unsuccessfully opposed the entrance of United Missouri Bancshares into the downtown financial district by maintaining that the depressed downtown could not support another bank. Rapid expansion and the continued profitability of the main bank, United Missouri Bank of Kansas City, pushed the total assets of the holding company over $1 billion in 1975, followed the next year by another milestone when it achieved $10 million in net income.

Opening of the downtown Saint Louis bank in January 1974 inaugurated a publicity gimmick that evolved into an integral part of the bank's advertising program until the idea fell into disfavor. The stunt required employees of the Saint Louis bank, including new bank president John Prentis, to parade through the downtown streets behind a 450-pound tiger cub named Czar. The bank's advertising agency made the tiger a new

corporate symbol to be used along with the insignia of three nested-letter *U*'s. The omnipresent tiger showed up at bank openings, was featured in advertisements, and attended bank board meetings for publicity shots. At bank openings, Crosby, Jr. led the tiger around the new facility; but the banker never felt comfortable as a tiger tamer. "I didn't like any part of it," said Crosby, Jr. "They all said everything's fine, don't worry, he's well trained. I don't think you can ever 'well train' a tiger." At one bank opening, Crosby, Jr. led the tiger through the front door to be greeted by a band playing "Dixie." The tiger suddenly leaned back on its haunches and roared loudly; Crosby, Jr. thought he had had it.

Advertising emphasized that United Missouri Bank was a "new breed of cat" in banking, but response to the new corporate symbol within the bank and in various markets was weak. Moreover, the tiger trademark posed another problem, since it also was the University of Missouri's symbol. The university did not particularly mind, but loyal alumni of other state universities and colleges who were good customers of United Missouri banks were not so favorably inclined to the bank's Mizzou tiger. The bank reemphasized its use of the nested-*U* corporate symbol.

The downtown Saint Louis bank also provides a wonderful gallery for United Missouri Bancshares' growing collection of American art. The interior of the United Missouri Bank of Saint Louis resembles a nineteenth-century English counting house and features dark wooden fixtures, grandfather clocks, antiques, and first-rate portraits by American artists. The variety of fine artwork reflects a great love and a life-long passion of Crosby Kemper, Jr. His father had cared little for art; but Crosby, Jr.'s grandmother Lottie, his mother Enid, and his uncle William had indulged their passion for art by becoming well-informed collectors. The interest in art extended to

being major patrons and supporters of the Nelson-Atkins Museum of Art and the Kansas City Art Institute.

Over the years, Crosby, Jr. assembled an outstanding corporate art collection that is highly regarded as one of the finest in the Midwest. By 1986, the collection included more than 500 pieces that reflect his own eclectic taste in art. Besides the early American portraits, the collection includes paintings by regionalists Andrew and James Wyeth, and Thomas Hart Benton; modern works by Roy Lichenstein, Andy Warhol, and Alexander Calder; a collection of Hopi Kachina dolls; and several paintings by southwestern artists of the Taos, New Mexico, school.

United Missouri Bank of Kansas City, in its capacity as the corporate trustee for the estate of Thomas Hart Benton, is custodian of perhaps the finest collection of paintings, drawings, and cartoons by the painter who lived the last forty years of his life in Kansas City. The extensive collection provided the basis for the 1985 publication of a major book by Karal Ann Marling about the regionalist painter, titled *Tom Benton and His Drawings: A Biographical Essay and a Collection of His Sketches, Studies, and Mural Cartoons*. Serious Benton scholars regularly ask United Missouri Bank of Kansas City for permission to study the artwork in detail or to reproduce artwork from the collection officially known as the Thomas Hart Benton and Rita P. Benton Testamentary Trusts. Crosby, Jr., who collected American realists, had acquired several Benton paintings and drawings for display in bank lobbies and offices. Just prior to the painter's death, Crosby, Jr. and Benton had discussed having the artist paint a mural that was to have been prominently displayed in the planned new bank headquarters. With a handshake, the two agreed on a price of $25,000; however, the eighty-six-year-old Benton died before beginning the work.

United Missouri Bancshares was developing a strong corporate identity. Each of the affiliate banks had a common name and a corporate symbol that was gaining public recognition. Internally, the holding company was providing strong support services for the affiliate banks in electronic data processing and through assistance from the Kansas City trust and bond departments. The Kemper approach to banking—personal service, high-quality loans, and aggressive marketing—that had built a highly successful, strong, and profitable Kansas City bank was being conveyed to the newly acquired affiliate banks.

During a sixty-year period, Crosby, Sr. and his son had established a strong tradition of successful banking, which provided United Missouri Bancshares with a remarkable degree of continuity and focus notably lacking in most other banks of similar size where periodic management changes were quite common. "Although the economy and the banking industry were not good in 1975," the cover of that year's annual report stated, "United Missouri flourished. We maintained a position of flexibility. We continued an intelligent lending policy proven by success. Our policy of investing in relatively short-term securities produced both healthy liquidity and healthy earnings, and we actively prospected for new deposits."

Senior bank officers, even twenty years later, still had vivid memories of how Crosby, Sr. used to run discount meetings to decide when and on what terms to loan money. The banker had been able to quickly size up a financial statement and sometimes had declared of the prospective borrower: "He's broke, world without end." When commercial-loan officers had presented loan proposals for various franchises, Crosby, Sr. often had responded with the statement that "It sounds like pee-wee golf to me," because he remembered banks having made bad loans on miniature golf courses in the 1930s and 1940s. Crosby, Sr. had always reminded his officers that banking was a "nose-to-nose, handshake-to-handshake business."

The lessons endured under Crosby, Jr. as he was very much like his father when it came to banking. Both had strong views about why they had been able to build a major financial institution. A seven-word phrase in one annual report captured the essence: "What worked for us before, worked again." The bank had grown remarkably as it had evolved into a statewide holding company, but it still placed a premium on personal relationships. Crosby, Jr. and top bank officers still made personal calls on major customers, maintained an open door to visitors, and answered their own phones.

Operation of the holding company required a great degree of delegated authority. One who had been given a great deal of authority was John Kramer. The affable banker, who had gone to work at City National Bank and Trust in 1937, had become instrumental in the formation of the holding company because of the many contacts and personal relationships he had cultivated during years of work in the correspondent banking department. In 1971, Kramer had been made president of the bank holding company, replacing Crosby, Jr., who had retained the title of chairman of the board. To Kramer had fallen the endless task of integrating the far-flung banks into a cohesive statewide banking organization.

Adding new banks to the holding company was not always as easy as the acquisition of the four banks that Kramer and Crosby, Jr. had corralled during their week-long trip in 1969. As a matter of principle, United Missouri Bancshares did not engage in unfriendly acquisitions; but adhering to that policy left the bank in a position of wanting to enter certain markets, yet being unable to acquire a bank that it considered worth buying or that was friendly to selling. In some instances, United Missouri Bancshares was left with little choice other than to open its own new bank.

United Missouri Bancshares had desperately wanted to have a bank in Jefferson City, the Missouri state capital. The Carthage-marble state capitol overlooking the Missouri River contained the office of the state treasurer, which controlled millions of dollars in state taxes, fees, and revenues. The main beneficiary of the lush source of deposits for years had been Jefferson City banks controlled by the family of Sam Cook, a prominent Democrat and third-generation banker. When United Missouri Bancshares had applied to the Comptroller of the Currency for a new Jefferson City bank charter, Cook's banks went to court to block granting of the new charter, which the Comptroller had approved August 13, 1973. The court petition

In 1972, United Missouri acquired Manufacturers and Mechanics Bank of Kansas City and built a new facility for the bank, which was renamed United Missouri Bank of Blue Valley.

claimed that "the predominant reason for applicant's desire to open a bank in Jefferson City is to exploit what they consider to be a deposit-rich market area. . . ." United Missouri Bancshares had been able to show that the high per-capita level of deposits in Jefferson City, low loan-to-deposit ratio, and high service charges justified chartering a new bank in the state capital to promote additional competition. United Missouri Bancshares had obtained the charter and in 1974 had opened a new bank with $1 million in capital that had been housed in a temporary 1,100-square-foot structure until the permanent building had been completed in 1975. Establishing United Missouri Bank of Jefferson City had proved to be an important decision, because it gave the state capital a physical banking presence with access to the investment banking and data-processing services maintained by the holding company in Kansas City. That combination, plus efficient service, eventually enabled United Missouri Bancshares to break the half-century stranglehold of the Cook family banks on the state government's major bank deposits.

United Missouri also had moved to strengthen its position in the Kansas City metropolitan area. Noticing the rapid residential development, United Missouri Bancshares in 1972 had made an unsuccessful effort to purchase the $5-million Bank of Jacomo in Blue Springs, which had been chartered just two years prior. The state banking commissioner, who had opposed the sale because he thought United Missouri Bancshares had offered to pay too high a premium for the bank, had raised objections that resulted in denial of the application by the Federal Reserve. The decision really perturbed Crosby, Jr.: "If United Missouri were stifling competition, that would

United Missouri Bank of Springfield, Missouri

The United Missouri banking facility at State Line and I-435 includes the EBT Restaurant, so named because the decor highlights historic artifacts that were salvaged when the bank demolished Emery, Bird, Thayer in 1972. Demolition of the Romanesque building designed by Henry Van Brunt sorely disappointed historic preservationists, who had the department store nominated for the National Register of Historic Places earlier that year.

have been one thing; but I don't see where the Federal Reserve has the right to determine what we want to pay for a bank." Still thinking that Blue Springs represented a good market, United Missouri Bancshares had immediately applied for a new national charter, which was granted in 1974. United Missouri also had been thwarted when its 1973 application to acquire the $36-million Westport Bank had been denied by the Federal Reserve on the premise that the acquisition could result in restricted banking competition in the area.

The company had been eager to establish a stronger presence in southern Kansas City where residential growth, upper-income neighborhoods, and business development offered greater opportunities for building a large deposit base. In 1973, United Missouri Bancshares had acquired the $27.2-million Hickman Mills Bank and Trust, which became United Missouri Bank of Hickman Mills through an exchange of stock, and also had acquired the $25.3-million Wornall Bank. The bank facilities at Seventy-Ninth Street and Wornall Road were immediately remodeled; and, at the same time, a new modern 36,000-square-foot building at 9201 Ward Parkway was constructed. When they were completed, the two offices were renamed United Missouri Bank South.

In 1977, United Missouri made one other strategic move in the Kansas City market by constructing a 53,000-square-foot bank facility at State Line Road and Interstate 435 that was to operate as a branch of United Missouri Bank of Kansas City. Literally right next to the Kansas border, the four-story branch facility was quite accessible to the major office boom underway along the interstate beltway, even though most of the development was occurring on the Kansas side.

The success of the new facility propelled the downtown bank to a

United Missouri Bank of Paris, Missouri

milestone that many long-time bank employees never thought they would live to see. For decades, the bank had run a poor third in Kansas City when compared in size to Commerce Trust and First National Bank; but when the Kansas City banks filed their financial statements on December 31, 1980, United Missouri Bank of Kansas City had edged past its two competitors to become the largest bank in the city, based on total resources of $1.18 billion. Crosby, Jr. confessed: "When I first joined United Missouri, then City National Bank, in January of 1950, I never thought in my lifetime I would see it grow to surpass all other banks in Kansas City."

In 1980, Crosby, Jr. proved himself a bold banking maverick who was willing to break ranks from the inexorable upward lockstep march of interest rates that were being set by the nation's money-center banks. At the annual meeting, United Missouri Bancshares announced that it was lowering its prime rate immediately; and it continued to do so throughout the year. Just two days before Christmas, United Missouri took the extraordinary measure of dropping its prime lending rate a full 1.5 percentage points from 21.5 percent, the record-high rate being charged by the money-center banks in New York City, Chicago, and California. Within two weeks, most of the major money-center banks matched the 20-percent prime lending rate at United Missouri, whereupon the Kansas City-based bank lowered its rate to 19.5 percent.

Money-center banks had long been viewed by Crosby, Jr. as no great paragon of banking wisdom. He firmly believed that strong regional banking companies, like United Missouri Bancshares, could offer a prime rate lower than the money-center banks, which had incurred substantial losses through foreign lending and real-estate investment trusts. "We wanted to bring the prime rate down," Crosby, Jr. said of the 1980 interest-rate reduc-

Versailles, *(1978)*
watercolor, 54x59¼ in.,
Fran Bull

tions. "When rates get high, nothing happens. Housing shuts down, and there isn't any capital formation. Lowering the prime interest rate was very important to us. A lot of our small business customers were really suffering, and we just thought we ought to be doing that as long as we had the [interest] spread." Cutting the prime received extensive national attention; and Crosby, Jr., for his efforts, received the Small Business Administration's Banker Advocate of the Year Award during a White House ceremony.

Cutting the prime was a classic move that reflected many of the cornerstones on which Crosby, Jr. and his father had built a major regional bank. First, a bank does not grow if its customers are being hurt by high interest rates. Second, a regional bank can compete effectively with money-

center banks in some areas but not by blindly following the lead of money-center banks in matters such as setting the prime rate. Third, paying high interest rates to get deposits, such as the purchase of other banks' surplus funds, only pushes up the loan rates. Fourth, poor lending practices by a bank often result in other customers having to pay for the mistakes. Fifth, being a bigger bank is of some importance; but it does not always mean that the bigger bank is better. Sixth, a hands-on approach by top officers is the preferred method to manage a bank.

Despite his community involvements, Crosby, Jr. remained intimately involved with bank affairs. He insisted on reviewing all real-estate loans handled by the bank. When widespread agricultural problems developed starting in 1984, Crosby, Jr. personally reviewed the loan portfolios of the holding company's small rural banks. "I believe in knowing what's going on," he said of his close attention to bank details, which often meant staying late at the office after other employees had gone home. Crosby, Jr. expected the same hands-on management by his top bank officers. "We cannot and will not countenance a willy-nilly operation," Crosby, Jr. had written in a strongly worded letter in 1971 to the president of a United Missouri affiliate bank who was not paying enough attention to banking business. "In order to have the right kind of operation, the top man must attend to details and set that kind of example; otherwise, you will find there will be serious mistakes made." The seventy-nine-year-old Crosby, Sr. had sent a memorandum the following day to congratulate his son on his "excellent" letter, which he hoped would "obtain the desired results."

Crosby, Jr.'s already strong ownership interest was virtually doubled because of two acquisitions made by United Missouri Bancshares. First came the July 1979 purchase of the United Missouri Mortgage Company, formerly the City Bond and Mortgage Company, which legally had been separated from the bank in 1934. The purchase was accomplished through an exchange of common stock that converted Crosby, Jr.'s substantial stock in the mortgage company into additional shares in United Missouri Bancshares. The story was repeated when United Missouri Bancshares in 1981 acquired City Bancshares, a one-bank holding company consisting of City Bank and Trust, which formerly had been the Grand Avenue Bank.

His controlling interest in City Bank and Trust had given Crosby, Jr. extensive influence over the policies of the bank that he had headed from 1964 to 1966. Crosby, Jr. and Lyle Wells, president of City Bank and a college-fraternity brother of Crosby, Jr.'s, had appropriated *The Scout* as the City Bank symbol after it had been dropped by United Missouri Bank of Kansas City and the holding company. Then in 1972, the bank had moved into an ultramodern facility in the newly developed Crown Center complex, just blocks south of the bank's Eighteenth and Grand location.

The close proximity of United Missouri Bank of Kansas City to City Bank and Trust Company had caused some problems for Crosby, Jr., the management of United Missouri Bancshares, and the directors. Both banks were competing in the same retail market; and United Missouri Bancshares

Model for Enterprise,
(1953) cast bronze,
Jacques Lipchitz

was anxious to strengthen its position in the Kansas City market, particularly since Saint Louis holding companies were actively moving into Kansas City. Crosby, Jr. was in the awkward position of wanting City Bank to be acquired by United Missouri Bancshares but was willing to entertain offers from other banks. Arriving at a fair purchase price for City Bank was difficult. An agreement was worked out in 1981 that involved exchanging more than 569,000 shares of United Missouri Bancshares stock for shares held by stockholders of City Bancshares. Because he had inherited some bank stock from his grandfather William Kemper, borrowed money to purchase controlling interest in the Grand Avenue Bank, and received stock exchanges for holding-company acquisitions, Crosby, Jr. had been able to gain nearly a 20-percent interest in United Missouri Bancshares, by then an institution with $2.3 billion in total assets. That was approximately the same ownership interest his father had held during his lifetime with the bank.

In 1985, the fifty-eight-year-old Crosby, Jr. decided that he wanted to retire from banking at age sixty-five, unlike his father who had strenuously resisted retirement until well into his seventies. Crosby, Jr.'s announcement came in conjunction with the appointment of Malcolm Aslin as president and chief executive officer of United Missouri Bank of Kansas City. Aslin, a thirty-seven-year-old University of Missouri business administra-

tion graduate, had joined the bank in 1972 as a trust officer. He was president of United Missouri Bank South from 1978 until he became president of the holding company in 1982. As the apparent successor upon Crosby, Jr.'s retirement, Aslin has demonstrated that he is clearly committed to steering the bank along the same course set by the two Kempers, whose ideas have become so firmly imbued within the organization. "We're saying the basics have been right for a lot of years, and our vision hasn't changed," said Aslin. "We don't do it with an eye shade and a quill pen any more, but we still balance every night. The terminology may be a little different, but we're still trying to maintain high quality assets, not just trying to put on loans."

Strong internal growth and additional acquisitions were pushing United Missouri Bancshares past new milestones. In 1975, sixty-two years following the founding of the little City Center Bank, United Missouri Bancshares topped $1 billion in total assets. The $2-billion mark was reached in just five additional years, and the $3-billion mark was exceeded in another five years. Aslin looked at the growth, the high earnings, and the bank's solid financial condition as self-evident proof that "clearly there is a place for a high-quality bank that knows its niche and can provide services in an exceptional manner."

One consideration in Crosby, Jr.'s desire to mold a strong management team had been his increasing role in civic affairs. Having overcome the disappointment of the UMKC performing-arts-center debacle, he had succeeded in raising funds for construction of a major downtown hotel. Downtown Kansas City seriously needed a major downtown convention hotel, but backers of the hotel project had been unable to put together a workable financial package to underwrite construction of a twenty-two-story hotel at Twelfth Street and Wyandotte that was to be called the Vista International Hotel. Prospects for construction of the hotel had improved when the United States Department of Housing and Urban Development had dangled a $10-million grant in front of the city and the developers, if the remaining $43 million for the project could be raised privately.

Despite the considerable federal carrot, Kansas City business leaders had been unable to produce their portion of the money, having developed local commitments of only $10 million. In late 1981, the project had seemed doomed after a $33-million loan commitment from the Union Labor Life Insurance Company of New York had fallen through. Crosby, Jr. had stepped in, hoping to replace the $33 million with local commitments before the federal grant was withdrawn. On December 18, 1981, he had dictated a terse letter that had been mailed to several of Kansas City's leading corporations and banks. The business leaders had been spared any pleasantries, and the banker had told them to "quit the hand-wringing and get something done." Crosby, Jr. had pledged $3 million from the Enid and Crosby Kemper Foundation, to which United Missouri Bank of Kansas City had added another $3 million. Within two days of mailing the letter, $11 million in loan commitments had been received and $22 million by week's end. Before he was through, Crosby, Jr. had secured loan or equity pledges totaling nearly

Crosby Kemper, Jr.'s community efforts became the fitting subject of a satirical April Fool's Day editorial in a local newspaper: "Crosby Kemper, who has already bailed out the Philharmonic and raised money for the new downtown hotel, has come to the aid of his city once more—in a more generous way than ever before. In a surprise press conference at City Hall, Mr. Kemper has announced that he was providing funds to give solvency to the Kansas City Kings, the Kansas City Comets, the Folly Theatre, the Kansas City Ballet, TWA, Computicket, Isis Foods and the City of Kansas City. . . . It is not known if Mr. Kemper will accept the city council's offer to rename the city, Kemper City."

Twin Houses, *(1969)*
watercolor, 21x29 in.,
Jamie Wyeth

Taos Pueblo,
oil, 17½x23½ in.,
Ralph Love

$35 million from Kansas City banks, businesses, and charitable trusts. "It seemed like an awesome task to raise the money locally," said Crosby, Jr., "but the hotel was a symbolic thing. It would have been a monumental failure, a terrible omen had we failed." Herman Sutherland, a bank director for forty years, said that Crosby, Jr.'s commitment to an issue occasionally

reached such an intensity that "he's so convinced he's right that he doesn't see anything wrong with being a little blunt."

*S*uch had been the case when it appeared that the Kansas City business community was going to let the Kansas City Philharmonic fail during the 1981–82 season. Crosby, Jr. no sooner had raised the money for the Vista International Hotel than he had stepped in to bail out the city's orchestra. The Philharmonic Association, in February 1982, had decided to cancel the remainder of the musical season, because it had been unable to raise $800,000 to cover an anticipated deficit. About an hour-and-a-half before cancellation of the season was to have been announced, Crosby, Jr. had offered to underwrite any debts incurred by the orchestra through financial support from United Missouri Bancshares, the family's charitable trust, and his own personal resources. "The conventional wisdom, unfortunately, was that it couldn't be saved and shouldn't be supported," said Crosby, Jr., who had worked diligently for the orchestra as a long-time philharmonic board member. The Kansas City Philharmonic had folded that year, but not without the formation of an entirely new Kansas City Symphony that was strongly supported by Crosby, Jr. As president of the symphony, he had headed a drive to raise a $10-million endowment fund that would yield sufficient income to meet the symphony's annual operating budget. The Enid and Crosby Kemper Charitable Trust had contributed $1 million, United Missouri Bancshares had pledged another $750,000, and Crosby, Jr. personally had added $250,000 to the endowment.

Crosby, Jr.'s efforts on behalf of the Vista International Hotel and the Kansas City Philharmonic had prompted a generous and glowing editorial about "The Banker" in the *Kansas City Star* in May 1982. "It used to be said constantly that Kansas City was going to pot because the skinflint bankers never did anything," said the editorial, which acknowledged Crosby, Jr.'s instrumental role in the hotel and orchestra. The success in saving those two projects, to many in the community, seemed to indicate a renewed civic pride in Kansas City. "There is further evidence of the Kemper feeling for Kansas City all over town—in the Nelson Gallery, for example, and, of course, the awesome outlines of the great Kemper Arena," the editorial added. "These are things to remember the next time you hear that the city's conservative bankers are ruining the town."

Despite his publicly proclaimed miracles in saving the Vista International Hotel and the Kansas City Philharmonic, Crosby, Jr. was quite bothered because his bank still had not constructed a new headquarters, one that would make a physical corporate statement about downtown Kansas City. The fresh-faced Aslin still remembers walking up Grand Avenue in 1972 for a job interview with the bank. Passing the Emery, Bird, Thayer site, he had noticed that his prospective employer had big plans, if the wooden sign was any indication. The sign had read: "Future Home of City National Bank." More than twelve years had elapsed, but Crosby, Jr. had not abandoned his plans to turn the expensive asphalt parking lot into a stunning new bank headquarters.

~8~

United Missouri Bank
STICKING TO THE BASICS

United Missouri Bank

The pounding jackhammers made quick work of the asphalt parking lot and provided an informal, but effective, groundbreaking for the planned building that had been discussed, debated, tabled, revived, and modified by United Missouri Bancshares over the previous decade. Finally, in the summer of 1984, the bank was beginning construction of a new headquarters on the lot bounded by Grand Avenue, Eleventh and Walnut streets in downtown Kansas City.

A parking lot was not what the bank had in mind in 1971 when it had acquired the prime piece of downtown real estate just a block south of its main bank at Tenth Street and Grand Avenue. The bank had not wanted to sell the land, but neither had it been prepared to construct a major multimillion-dollar headquarters at the time. Since abandoning plans to build was out of the question, Crosby Kemper, Jr. had declared periodically that the bank was ready to build its new headquarters; though details and a construction timetable had not been worked out.

Formal announcement of the new bank headquarters came in May 1984 when Crosby Kemper, Jr. stated, "With the rapid expansion of our bank in the past few years, the new building is essential if we are to continue to grow and to provide quality service to our customers." The plans were less grandiose than Pei's 1973 design that had been rejected by the bank as impractical and too expensive. The new plan, designed by Abend-Singleton Associates, Inc., reflected Pei's earlier concerns about maintaining open space and not competing in height or bulk with surrounding buildings. The architects selected polished, ruby-red granite and tinted green glass for the exterior of the 255,800-square-foot building, which wraps around an open courtyard extending northeast from the corner of Eleventh and Walnut streets. The structure has an asymmetric shape with six floors on the Grand Avenue side and three floors on the Walnut Street side. The building design anticipates the possible addition of a twenty-five-story tower with 500,000 square feet adjacent to Walnut Street. "If we could find a tenant, we would build it," Crosby, Jr. said, "but we don't feel that a bank should be heavily into the speculative office market." Even before a concrete footing was poured, the bank had leasing commitments for all of the space not intended

for bank use. The new building affords sufficient space for the bank to locate all of its core customer-contact services—personal banking, bonds, trust, commercial loans, and safe-deposit boxes—within the same facility. A covered pedestrian walkway connects the new headquarters with the R. A. Long Building, where bank operations are to be consolidated.

The bank and architects adhered to Pei's earlier concept of making the building "an oasis in downtown, a garden in the center" where pedestrians could stop to relax away from sidewalks and streets. On Crosby, Jr.'s recommendation, the bank commissioned an abstract bronze sculpture by New York artist Nancy Graves, who is quite enthusiastic about the courtyard location for her large sculpture. But over and above the aesthetic appeal, the new building is an important symbol to the community. "I felt that we needed to make a statement that we are growing with the city," said Malcolm Aslin, president of the bank holding company, who had pushed for construction of the new headquarters. The building, besides solving space problems, was a multimillion-dollar, brick-and-mortar reaffirmation of a long-held tenet of the Kemper-run bank: "It's great to grow with the City."

Evidence of the company's growth had been spread across the pages of its annual reports. Each year, United Missouri Bancshares invariably had reported new records for net income, deposits, or total assets. The company, which had twenty-two affiliate banks and counted total deposits of $2.4 billion dollars at the end of 1985, credited its success to a basic company philosophy: "We emphasize quality and concentrate on doing what we know how to do and doing it well." This seventeen-word phrase, worthy of being chiseled into stone, explains why United Missouri Bancshares has remained a profitable, growing company. In 1985, a post-Depression record of 120 banks failed—nearly half within a day's drive of Kansas City—but United Missouri did well by sticking to the basics: looking for quality loans and market niches where it was able to offer excellent services while earning fee-based income.

United Missouri Bancshares remained a strong, solvent bank holding company that had avoided fiscal irresponsibility, as evidenced in two 1985 and 1986 nationwide studies of the banking industry. Veribanc, Inc., well-respected bank analysts, evaluated the nation's 14,000 banks using computer analyses of balance sheets and income statements. The analysts produced a list of 900 commercial banks that qualified as "blue banks," extremely strong banks, because the banks met each of these criteria: equity ratio of 7.5 percent or better, liquidity ratio of more than 45 percent, and a return on assets of 1 percent or more for the previous two fiscal quarters. United Missouri Bank of Kansas City, with assets of $1.15 billion, was the largest blue bank in Missouri in a state-by-state listing. The second study, completed by Sheshunoff and Company, gave United Missouri Bank of Kansas City its highest rating, an *A+*, based on 1985 financial figures. Banks were awarded an *A+* rating if they scored 90 points or more on the composite numerical rating system that evaluated capital adequacy, quality of assets, earnings, liquidity, problem loans, and bank growth. United Missouri Bank

of Kansas City received 99 out of 100 points. "Obviously, we're happy to receive the rating, but we expect that of ourselves," Aslin said.

*A*slin had quickly underscored the importance of excellence in his first months as Crosby, Jr.'s apparent successor. The occasion was the annual United Missouri Bancshares management conference attended by the bank's top officers. "We work for an excellent company, a company that is generally recognized for the quality of its assets, the quality of its services, and the quality of its earnings over the year," Aslin said. "We are not planning a new direction, we are merely recognizing some of the traits that have led to our excellence. . . ." The traits, he said, provided an enduring "model for excellence." Aslin then cited a dozen objectives that he considered important to the bank's continuing excellence: maximize return on shareholders' equity; be a market-driven, not a product-driven company; deliver quality in the development and delivery of products; maintain high ethical standards; develop employee pride; promote better communications; foster teamwork; be a good corporate citizen; maintain buildings and grounds; develop employee skills; make strategic plans; and recognize and reward employee excellence.

Doing the basics well accounted for two major developments during 1985. First, United Missouri Bancshares took advantage of its tremendous data-processing capabilities and its extensive experience in corporate cash management to put together a successful bid to handle the State of Missouri's banking. The state had not moved its major accounts in fifty-three years, but the move to United Missouri was going to save the state nearly $2 million in bank fees. State Treasurer Wendall Bailey credited United Missouri with improved collection methods and earlier availability of funds that increased the state's daily balances by about $12 million, on which the state could earn $1 million in interest income annually.

The second development was the establishment of United Missouri Trust Company of New York to improve the processing of extensive bond and securities dealings conducted by United Missouri Bank's trust department for individual and institutional clients. The bank opened the New York City office in the expensive financial district just two blocks from bustling Wall Street. On an average day during the first few months of operation, the New York office handled $500 to $600 million in securities, though totals topped $1 billion on the busiest days. United Missouri Bank had been dissatisfied with the poor service and high fees that it had been paying to third-party processing agents to handle these securities transactions.

In April 1986, the Missouri Legislature approved a regional banking law that permits banks in any of the eight adjoining states to establish banks in Missouri if that state allows out-of-state banking under a reciprocal agreement. Three states—Illinois, Tennessee, and Kentucky—have similar regional banking laws, and Oklahoma will be added to the list in 1987. Regional banking brought with it fundamental changes. Banks, once restricted to operating out of a single building, were able to expand into a multistate region larger than any European nation. United Missouri Bancshares

"Traditionally, banks like to say they are secure and strong and successful. So the profuse use of a material such as polished granite says this is an important building. I think it says strength. It says this is a member of the community that's a leader."

E. Crichton Singleton, *lead architect*
Abend Singleton Associates Inc.

adopted a very cautious approach toward moving across state lines. "It would be nice to get our name in the paper as being progressive and going across the [Mississippi] river," Aslin said. "I think it's more important to have the courage to stick with the convictions that have gotten the company to where it is today."

*H*oping to develop the Saint Louis market and with the prospects of interstate banking on the horizon, United Missouri Bancshares had progressively strengthened its Saint Louis banks. First, the Saint Louis banks had acquired their own in-house data-processing operations and had developed their own correspondent banking department to serve banks within the separate Saint Louis Federal Reserve District. Then the banks established their own trust department. In 1986, all of the affiliate Saint Louis metropolitan-area banks were merged into United Missouri Bank of Saint Louis with combined assets of $365 million. Many of the moves were in anticipation that United Missouri Bank of Saint Louis would assume direct management of any interstate bank acquisitions in south-central Illinois.

The financial analysts had speculated about United Missouri Bancshares' plans for the Saint Louis market when Kemper and the company quietly had begun buying up shares of Centerre Bancorporation stock in 1984. In March 1985, United Missouri Bancshares had applied to the Fed-

eral Reserve for approval to buy up to 10 percent of Centerre's outstanding stock. Many had thought that the Saint Louis-based Centerre—the state's third-largest bank holding company—might be acquired by United Missouri Bancshares through an unfriendly merger. United Missouri Bancshares had purchased about 345,000 Centerre shares—about 4.5 percent of the outstanding shares—which did not include another 5 percent owned by William Kemper, Jr., uncle of Crosby Kemper, Jr. The 10 percent owned by Kemper-family interests had been substantially more than the 2.2-percent stake held by Centerre's officers and directors.

United Missouri Bancshares had bought most of the Centerre stock for $25.00 to $26.25 a share, substantially lower than its book value of $40.00 per share. The low stock price relative to book value reflected the problem loans that had hurt Centerre's earnings. "We're just buying it as an investment because we think it's awfully cheap," Crosby, Jr. had said. As major stockholders, Crosby, Jr. and United Missouri Bancshares had pressed Centerre to burn the midnight oil to collect past-due loans and to cut overhead expenses. As Centerre's performance had improved, the stock price had climbed. United Missouri Bancshares had stopped purchasing shares but had gleefully watched its original investment grow. In August 1986, United Missouri Bancshares and the Kemper charitable trusts sold 150,000 shares of Centerre stock for at least twice their approximately $3.7 million original investment. "This was really an opportunity to sell a big block of stock and get

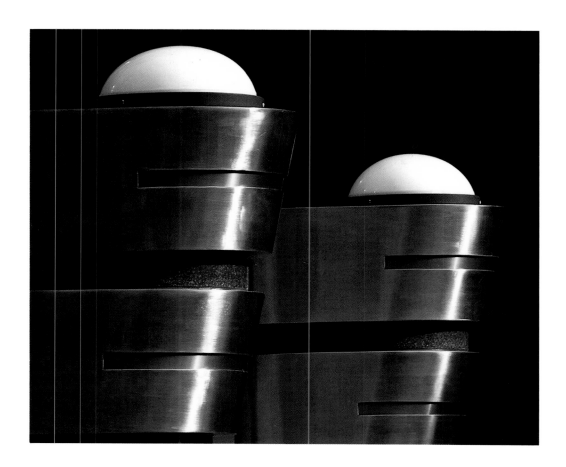

Each year, United Missouri
Bancshares holds a
Management Conference
where officers, department
heads, and top managers from
throughout the bank holding
company meet to discuss
financial trends, banking
legislation, marketing trends,
and growth of the company.
This group picture was taken at
the 1986 conference held in
Colorado Springs, Colorado.

our original investment out of it, so we have the money free for other things," Aslin said.

*A*t is scarcely conceivable that United Missouri Bancshares has evolved from the small bank where William Kemper had addressed the board of directors on April 16, 1918, about "the future policy of the bank." The bank's extraordinary success might seem unimaginable, even to a great dreamer like William Kemper. If permitted the pleasures of time travel, he might wander through the new headquarters of the bank run by his grandson, shaking his head in disbelief.

What would William Kemper have to say about the computers? Would he be surprised to read that his bank had been named to *Forbes'* list of the top 300 mid-size growth companies in the United States in 1983 and 1984? Would he believe that in 1985 the descendant of his one-story bank at 1728 Grand Avenue had issued 850,000 credit cards and processed more than $732 million in annual bankcard sales? Would he doubt published reports stating that in 1985 his little City Center Bank had grown to be so big and strong that it was ranked fourth in capital strength among the nation's top 300 banks by the *American Banker?* Would he be speechless to learn that in 1986 the bank's wire-transfer department handled an average of 2,900 transactions each day, moving an average of $3.5 billion? What would he think of the new bank headquarters, the cost of which exceeded the bank's total deposits in 1938, the year he had died?

Not easily fooled by appearances, William Kemper would probably stop at a bank officer's desk to ask for a copy of the latest annual report. Would he question the professional competency of the accountants? Surely the totals for 1985 could not be right—total assets, $2.9 billion; total deposits, $2.4 billion; and net income, $30.3 million. Could he venture to imagine what his father-in-law Rufus Crosby—the private banker on the Kansas prairie—might think of the impressive fiscal report? Or what his own son Crosby, Sr. might have to say?

Then perhaps he would smile and think back to his own start in banking at the Valley Falls Bank of Deposit in eastern Kansas. His son Crosby, Sr. and grandson Crosby, Jr.—two tall men in the banking business—simply had pursued with diligence, fervor, and consistency the same objective that private banker Rufus Crosby had set for himself in 1879 when he first went into banking: "Our steady purpose shall be to do all the various and legitimate kinds of business of a **First Class Bank,** on strict and true banking rules and regulations."

One family, in the intervening century, has accomplished that objective—not alone, but with the assistance of thousands of dedicated associates who had models of excellence to emulate. The bank has grown in grand style to the credit of the Kempers, the bank's staff, its customers, its directors, its stockholders, and the communities it serves. Indeed, this ongoing story of a remarkable bank is ample testimony to a simple truth: it has been great to grow with the city.

Dollar Bill, *(1962)*
crayon and watercolor,
30x40 in.,
Andy Warhol

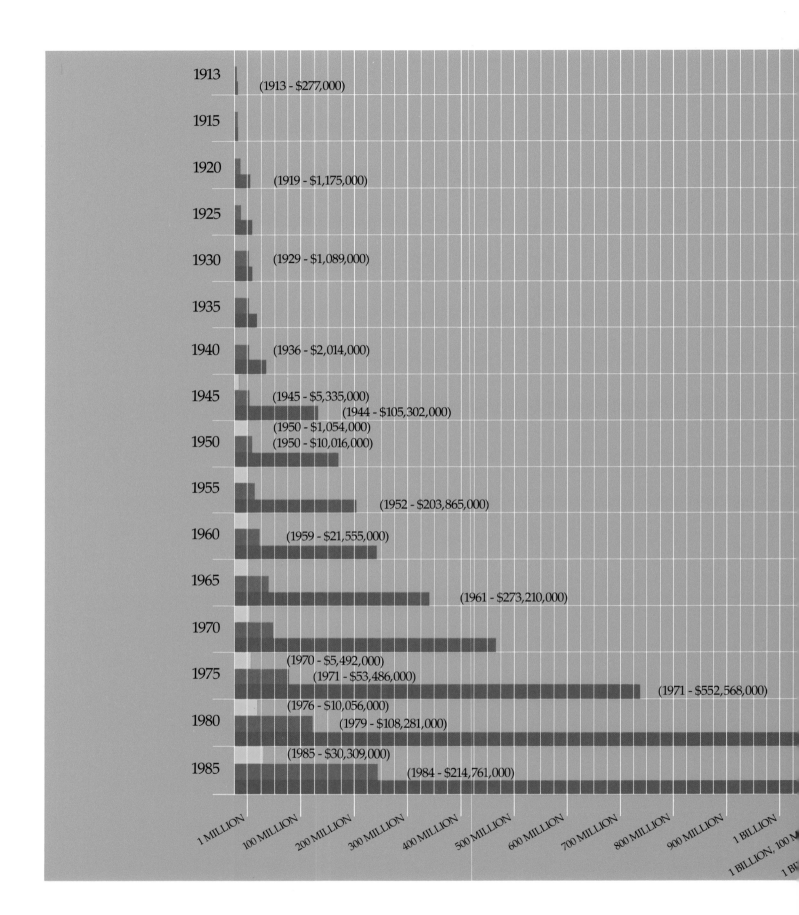

1913

(1913 - $277,000)

1915

1920

(1919 - $1,175,000)

1925

1930

(1929 - $1,089,000)

1935

1940

(1936 - $2,014,000)

1945

(1945 - $5,335,000)

(1944 - $105,302,000)

(1950 - $1,054,000)

1950

(1950 - $10,016,000)

1955

(1952 - $203,865,000)

1960

(1959 - $21,555,000)

1965

(1961 - $273,210,000)

1970

(1970 - $5,492,000)

1975

(1971 - $53,486,000)

(1971 - $552,568,000)

(1976 - $10,056,000)

1980

(1979 - $108,281,000)

(1985 - $30,309,000)

1985

(1984 - $214,761,000)

1 MILLION   100 MILLION   200 MILLION   300 MILLION   400 MILLION   500 MILLION   600 MILLION   700 MILLION   800 MILLION   900 MILLION   1 BILLION   1 BILLION, 100 M   1 BI

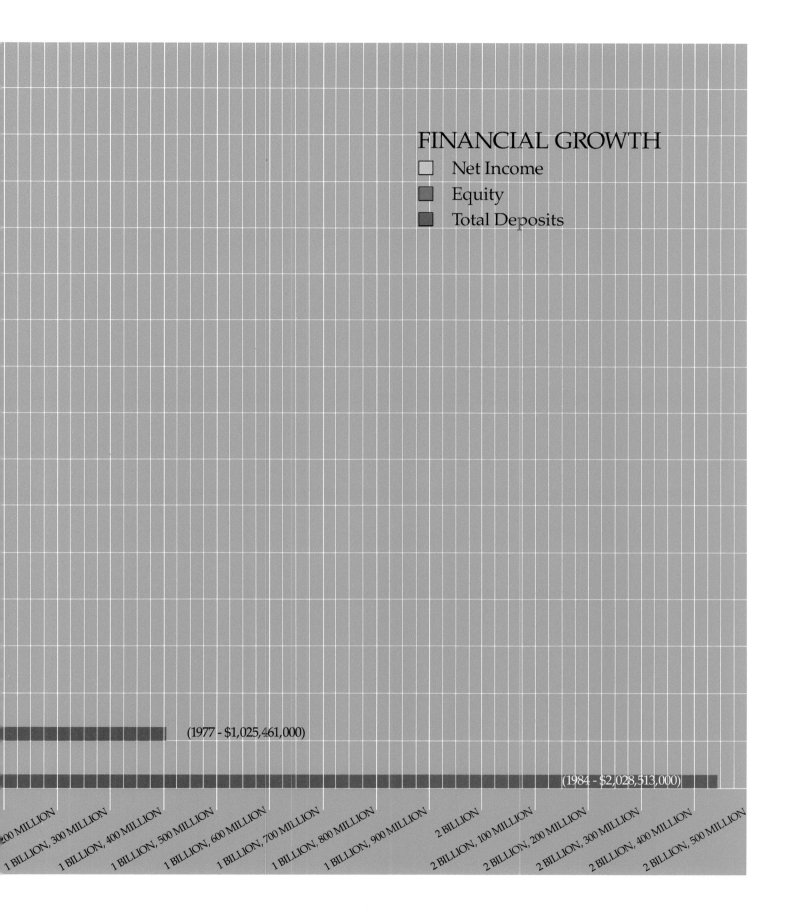

FINANCIAL GROWTH

☐ Net Income
■ Equity
■ Total Deposits

(1977 - $1,025,461,000)

(1984 - $2,028,513,000)

200 MILLION

1 BILLION, 300 MILLION

1 BILLION, 400 MILLION

1 BILLION, 500 MILLION

1 BILLION, 600 MILLION

1 BILLION, 700 MILLION

1 BILLION, 800 MILLION

1 BILLION, 900 MILLION

2 BILLION

2 BILLION, 100 MILLION

2 BILLION, 200 MILLION

2 BILLION, 300 MILLION

2 BILLION, 400 MILLION

2 BILLION, 500 MILLION

UNITED MISSOURI BANCSHARES, INC.
Chronological Growth

1969

Missouri Bancshares, Inc. holding company formed

City National Bank and Trust Company, chartered 1913
(Now United Missouri Bank of Kansas City, n.a.)

1970

Kemper State Bank, chartered 1928
(Now United Missouri Bank of Boonville)

The Central National Bank of Carthage, chartered 1890
(Now United Missouri Bank of Carthage)

Security National Bank of Joplin, chartered 1964
(Now United Missouri Bank of Joplin)

Peoples National Bank of Warrensburg, chartered 1898
(Now United Missouri Bank of Warrensburg)

1971

Name of holding company changed to United Missouri Bank, Inc.

First Security Bank in Kirkwood, chartered 1934
(Became United Missouri Bank of Kirkwood)

Arnold Savings Bank, chartered 1913
(Became United Missouri Bank of Jefferson County)

Bank of Ferguson, chartered 1906
(Became United Missouri Bank of Ferguson)

1972

Names of all affiliate banks changed to United Missouri Bank

United Missouri Bank of Brookfield
(Formerly The Brookfield Banking Company, chartered 1874)

United Missouri Bank of Blue Valley
(Formerly Manufacturers and Mechanics Bank of Kansas City, chartered 1911)

1973

United Missouri Bank South
(Formerly Wornall Bank, chartered 1955)

United Missouri Bank of Hickman Mills
(Formerly Hickman Mills Bank and Trust Co., chartered 1921)

United Missouri Bank of Saint Louis, n.a. (original charter)

1974

United Missouri Bank of Blue Springs (original charter)

United Missouri Bank of Springfield
(Formerly First City Bank of Springfield, chartered 1967)

United Missouri Bank of Jefferson City (original charter)

United Missouri Bank of Milan
(Formerly The First National Bank of Milan, chartered 1884)

1976

United Missouri Bank of Saint Joseph
(Formerly The Park Bank, chartered 1889)

United Missouri Bank of Monett
(Formerly Gillioz Bank and Trust Company, chartered 1934)

1978

United Missouri Bank of Cass County
(Formerly The Cass County Bank, chartered 1902)

1979

United Missouri Mortgage Company, a subsidiary of United Missouri Bancshares, Inc.
(Formerly City Bond and Mortgage Company, founded 1934)

1980

United Missouri Bank of Warsaw
(Formerly Community Bank of Warsaw, chartered 1934)

1981

United Missouri Mortgage Company, a subsidiary of United Missouri Bank of Kansas City, n.a.

1982

United Missouri Bank of Paris
(Formerly The Paris Savings Bank, chartered 1885)

United Missouri City Bank
(Formerly City Bank and Trust Company and Grand Avenue Bank and Trust Company, chartered 1947)

United Missouri Bank Northland
(Formerly Platte County Bank of Camden Point, chartered 1889)

1983

United Missouri Banks of Blue Springs and Blue Valley
(Merged into United Missouri City Bank)

1984

United Missouri Capital Corporation
(Founded as a subsidiary of United Missouri Bank of Kansas City, n.a.)

United Missouri Bank of Brookfield, Bucklin Office
(Formerly Bucklin State Bank, chartered 1925)

1985

United Missouri Bank of Saint Louis County, n.a.
(Formed through a merger of United Missouri Banks of Ferguson and Kirkwood)

United Missouri Bank of Linn County
(Formerly Linn County State Bank, chartered 1896)

United Missouri Bank of Saint Joseph, Clarksdale Office
(Formerly The Clarksdale Bank, chartered 1927)

1986

United Missouri Banks of St Louis and Jefferson County
(Merged into United Missouri Bank of Saint Louis County,
which became United Missouri Bank of Saint Louis, n.a.)

United Missouri Bank North Central
(Formed through a merger of United Missouri Banks of Brookfield and Linn County)

United Missouri Brokerage Services, Inc.
(Founded as a subsidiary of United Missouri Bancshares, Inc.)

United Missouri Bancshares, Inc. and United Missouri Bank of Kansas City, n.a.
(New corporate headquarters constructed at 1010 Grand Avenue)

United Missouri Bank of Saint Joseph, Albany Office
(Formerly Albany State Bank, chartered 1980)

United Missouri Bank of Saint Joseph, Mound City and Maitland Offices
(Formerly Missouri Farmers Bank, chartered 1934)

Affiliate Banks

United Missouri Bank of Boonville

United Missouri Bank of Carthage

United Missouri Bank of Cass County

United Missouri City Bank
Offices in Blue Springs and Kansas City

United Missouri Bank of Hickman Mills

United Missouri Bank of Jefferson City

United Missouri Bank of Joplin

United Missouri Bank of Kansas City, n.a.

United Missouri Bank of Milan

United Missouri Bank of Monett

United Missouri Bank North Central
Offices in Brookfield, Bucklin, Laclede, and Linneus

United Missouri Bank Northland
Offices in Camden Point and northland Kansas City

United Missouri Bank of Paris

United Missouri Bank of Saint Joseph
Offices in Albany, Clarksdale, Faucett, Maitland, Mound City, and Saint Joseph

United Missouri Bank of Saint Louis, n.a.
*Offices in Arnold, Central City, Clayton, Ferguson, Kirkwood,
Maryland Heights, downtown Saint Louis, and Town and Country*

United Missouri Bank South

United Missouri Bank of Springfield

United Missouri Bank of Warrensburg

United Missouri Bank of Warsaw